From the original by Gilbert Stuart after the engraving of H. B. Hall, Jr.

JAMES MADISON'S NOTES
OF DEBATES

IN THE

FEDERAL CONVENTION OF 1787

AND THEIR RELATION TO A MORE PER-
FECT SOCIETY OF NATIONS

BY

JAMES BROWN SCOTT

Technical Delegate of the United States to the Second Hague Peace
Conference; Member of the Institute of International Law;
President of the American Institute of International Law

THE LAWBOOK EXCHANGE, LTD.
Clark, New Jersey

ISBN 978-1-58477-164-7

Lawbook Exchange edition 2001, 2019

The quality of this reprint is equivalent to the quality of the original work.

THE LAWBOOK EXCHANGE, LTD.
33 Terminal Avenue
Clark, New Jersey 07066-1321

*Please see our website for a selection of our other publications
and fine facsimile reprints of classic works of legal history:*
www.lawbookexchange.com

Library of Congress Cataloging-in-Publication Data

Scott, James Brown, 1866-1943.
  James Madison's notes of debates in the Federal convention of 1787 and
their relation to a more perfect society of nations / by James Brown Scott.
    p. cm.
  Originally published: New York: Oxford University Press, American
Branch, 1918.
  Includes bibliographical references.
  ISBN 1-58477-164-X (cloth: alk. paper)
  1. Constitutional history--United States--Sources. 2. United States.
Constitutional Convention (1787) 3. Madison, James, 1751-1836 4. United
States. Constitution. I.
  Madison, James, 1751-1836. II. Title.

KF4520 .S37 2001
342.73'024--dc21   00-066331

Printed in the United States of America on acid-free paper

JAMES MADISON'S NOTES
OF DEBATES

IN THE

FEDERAL CONVENTION OF 1787

AND THEIR RELATION TO A MORE PER-
FECT SOCIETY OF NATIONS

BY

JAMES BROWN SCOTT

Technical Delegate of the United States to the Second Hague Peace
Conference ; Member of the Institute of International Law ;
President of the American Institute of International Law

NEW YORK
OXFORD UNIVERSITY PRESS
AMERICAN BRANCH: 35 WEST 32ND STREET
LONDON, TORONTO, MELBOURNE, AND BOMBAY
1918

TO

ARTHUR DEERIN CALL
THIS LITTLE BOOK IS AFFECTIONATELY
INSCRIBED

"Now a new strain, a new impulse, the strain and impulse of those who build and make good what they have achieved, was upon the leaders of the young States, and they spoke their chastened thought like masters." (Woodrow Wilson, *A History of the American People*, Ch. II, " Founding a Federal Government," Vol. III, p. 82, 1901.)

" What we seek is the reign of law, based upon the consent of the governed and sustained by the organized opinion of mankind." (President Wilson's *Address of July 4, 1918*, delivered at Mount Vernon.)

PREFACE

For years past the writer of this little book has been of the opinion that the Federal Convention of the States which formed the Constitution of the United States was in fact as well as in form an international conference. For this reason he is firmly convinced that the proceedings of the Convention are therefore of interest in this day of international conferences, as showing the steps by which the thirteen States of the western world, claiming to be sovereign, free and independent, were able to form the one large, successful and enduring union of States to be found in the annals of history.

Whether the Society of Nations will care to form a more perfect union of its members is for them alone to decide, but if they should care to strengthen the bonds that unite them and consciously to form an international organization, in which the States shall recognize their interdependence as well as their independence, Mr. Madison's Notes of the proceedings of the Federal Convention of 1787, in which that happy result was achieved, should be mastered and the experience of the United States under the more perfect union be taken into consideration.

In this connection it may be added that an edition of Mr. Madison's Notes, prepared by Mr.

Galliard Hunt and the undersigned, is in press, to which have been prefixed and appended the various documents requisite for a correct understanding of the nature and labors of the gathering, and which establish without argument or comment its international character, and its international value.

JAMES BROWN SCOTT,

WASHINGTON, D. C.
November 11, 1918.

TABLE OF CONTENTS

Table of Contents

ILLUSTRATIONS

JAMES MADISON—*Tabula Vitae*

Born, Port Conway, King George County, Virginia, March 16, 1751.

Graduated at Princeton, 1771.

Delegate to the Convention of Virginia, 1776.

Member of House of Delegates, 1776.

Member of Governor's Council, 1777.

Delegate to Continental Congress, 1780.

Member of House of Delegates, 1784.

Member to Annapolis Convention, 1786.

Delegate to Congress, 1787.

Member of Federal Convention, 1787.

Member of the Constitutional Convention of Virginia, 1788.

Member of House of Representatives, 1789-1797.

Member of the House of Delegates of Virginia, 1799.

Secretary of State of the United States during President Jefferson's Administration, 1801-1809.

President of United States, 1809-1817.

Delegate to the Constitutional Convention of Virginia, 1829.

Died, Montpelier, Orange County, Virginia, June 28, 1836.

BIBLIOGRAPHY OF MADISON'S NOTES OF DEBATES IN THE FEDERAL CONVENTION OF 1787

The Papers of James Madison, purchased by order of Congress; being his correspondence and reports of debates during the Congress of the confederation, and his reports of debates in the Federal Convention; now published from the original manuscripts, deposited in the Department of State, by direction of the Joint Library Committee of Congress, under the superintendence of Henry D. Gilpin. Washington, Langtree & O'Sullivan, 1840. 3 vols., facsim. Vol. 2-3. Debates in the Federal Convention of 1787. Vol. 2, pp. 683-1242; Vol. 3, pp. 1243-1264.
(Some copies of this edition have the imprint New York; J. & H. G. Langley, 1841, and others are dated Mobile, 1852. Still other copies were published in Boston.)

Debates on the Adoption of the Federal Constitution, in the Convention held at Philadelphia, in 1787; with a diary of the debates of the Congress of the Confederation; as reported by James Madison. Revised and newly arranged by Jonathan Elliot. Complete in one volume. Volume v. Supplementary to Elliot's Debates. Washington, printed for the Editor, 1845. xxii, p. 641.
(In 1853 the plates passed into the hands of J. B. Lippincott & Co., who have printed several editions, with change of date only.)

Journal of the Federal Convention kept by James Madison, Reprinted from edition of 1840, which was published under direction of the United States Government from the original manuscripts. Ed. by E. H. Scott. Special edition, Chicago, Albert, Scott & Co., 1893. 805 p.
(Another edition was published by Albert, Scott & Co. in 1893, in two volumes, and in 1898, Scott, Foresman and Company (Chicago) issued a two volume edition.)

Madison's Notes of the Proceedings of the Federal Convention. Washington, Dept. of State, 1900. 904 p.
Published as volume III of the Documentary History of the Constitution of the United States of America, 1787-1870, published by the Department of State, 1894-1905.

The Writings of James Madison, comprising his public papers and his private correspondence, including numerous letters and documents now for the first time printed. Ed. by Gaillard Hunt. New York [etc.], G. P. Putnam's Sons, 1900-10. 9 vols., illus., 6 facsim.

Vol. 3-4. 1787. The Journal of the Constitutional Convention. 1902-1903. Vol. 3-4, 471 p.; vol. 4, 551 p.

The Journal of the Debates in the Convention which framed the Constitution of the United States, May-September, 1787, as recorded by James Madison. Ed. by Gaillard Hunt. New York and London, G. P. Putanm's Sons, 1908. 2 vols., 5 facsim.

The Records of the Federal Convention of 1787. Ed. by Max Farrand. New Haven, Yale University Press [etc., etc.], 1911. 3 vols. Vol. 1-2. The Records of the Federal Convention of 1787.

JAMES MADISON'S NOTES OF DEBATES IN THE FEDERAL CONVENTION OF 1787 AND THEIR RELATION TO A MORE PERFECT SOCIETY OF NATIONS[1]

THE COLOSSAL TASK

The notes of debates in the Federal Convention, held in the city of Philadelphia in the State of Pennsylvania, from the 25th day of May to the 17th day of September, in the year of our Lord one thousand seven hundred eighty-seven, are notes which James Madison of Virginia, an eye witness and active participant, made from day to day, from hour to hour, and from minute to minute, of the proceedings of that gathering. The Convention was composed of official delegates of twelve of the thirteen " free, sovereign and independent States " of America forming an imperfect union or loose league under Articles of Confederation, which articles had been drafted during the war

A significant record of a significant event.

[1] The quotations from Mr. Madison's Notes are taken in every instance from volume III of *The Documentary History of the Constitution* containing them in the form in which they were left by the distinguished reporter and statesman.

As, however, Mr. Madison arranged his Notes chronologically, and as the reference in the text is made in each instance to the specific session and date thereof, any edition of the Notes may be used.

of the American Revolution by the delegates of the thirteen States in the Continental Congress, and ratified thereafter from time to time by their respective legislatures, and binding upon all when finally ratified by the last of the thirteen on March 1, 1781. From its origin and nature this body of official delegates was at the time generally known as the Federal Convention. It is now popularly termed the Constitutional Convention because its labors resulted in a Constitution intended for the thirteen, now binding upon the forty-eight political communities forming the United States of America. It was thus, in inception, nature and form, a conference; from the political point of view it was an American, from the geographical situation a continental, from the international aspect it was an international conference. The States represented in this conference formed, it may be said, a group apart from the Society of Nations and held only loosely together by their common consent. They were the product of a political philosophy in which the people of each State were the source of power within the State. They were separated by an ocean from the Old World. They had a continent within which to experiment. The experience of Europe was to them both a guide and a warning. With no obstacles to overcome but those of their own creation, no mistakes to correct but their own, they were faced with an opportunity unusual as it was significant. That we of to-day know how that opportunity was utilized is due to the painstaking care and unwavering devotion of James Madison.

Inasmuch as this assembly was an international conference—Mr. Madison himself calls it a "Federal Convention"—the instrument of gov- Scope of this inquiry. ernment which it framed and recommended to the Congress and the States for ratification, properly called a Federal Constitution, is an international document. It seems natural, therefore, that we should all in this period of international transition be interested to consider Mr. Madison and the manner in which he took the notes; to review the reasons which led the States to appoint delegates to confer in Philadelphia; to recount the difficulties met and overcome in compromising adverse and outwardly irreconcilable interests on the part of the States; to analyze the main provisions which the delegates in conference framed for a more perfect union of the several States, and to indicate in general how the Society of Nations can profit by the labors of this Federal Convention. If men be minded to create a more perfect Society of Nations and to endow it with agencies to carry into effect the terms of their agreement, they will be heartened by the history of these things, for, as the venerable Dr. Franklin said in speaking of the Convention, "We had many interests to reconcile."[1]

The man who took notes of the debates of the conference was ideally qualified for his self-

[1] Letter dated Philadelphia, October 22, 1787, from Benjamin Franklin to Mr. Grand. (*Documentary History of the Constitution*, published by the Department of State, vol. IV., pp. 341-342.)

imposed task, for, while neither the official Secretary nor the designated reporter of the conference, he was a delegate from Virginia, cognizant of the aims and purposes of the gathering which he, more than any man then living, had helped to bring about. As a member from Virginia of the Continental Congress, acting under and in accordance with the Articles of Confederation, he had learned to appreciate from practical experience the defects of the Articles, to amend which the conference had been called. He was personally acquainted with many of the leading figures of the conference, inasmuch as they had served together in the Congress, and he was therefore familiar with their style of speech and manner of speaking. Having abstracted the debates of the Congress in which they and he had participated, he was already a practiced reporter. Added to these personal and technical qualifications he was deeply impressed with the importance of the occasion; indeed, he had prepared himself by a careful and elaborate study of the defects of the government, or rather the lack of government under the Articles, and his " Observations " in which he recorded his views of those defects is today the most authentic and detailed survey of the subject from the pen of any contemporary statesman, publicist or chronicler. He had further prepared himself for the rôle which he was to play as a delegate by a study of all known instances of federation in so far as the scanty material then at hand would permit. He had finally fitted himself for that leadership in the conference accorded him by his fellow delegates from the first day of its proceedings, by drafting and submitting in advance the nature and scope of the amendments to be proposed, and also the " Plan " presented by the delegation of Virginia which served as the basis of discussion, and which, modified in principle and in form, became the Constitution of the perfected Union. But in addition, if indeed anything can be added, he went to the conference with the deliberate intention, formed in advance and carried out from day to day, of recording the proceedings and of taking down the debates in his system of original shorthand, in order that future students of Federal Government at least should have an authentic and adequate account of the Federal Convention of 1787.

We do not need to conjecture as to his intentions in these matters, to examine his formal writings, to search his personal correspondence or to bring together passages from different sources in order to establish these facts, as Mr. Madison has saved us the trouble by stating it all in express language and in detailed form in the preface which he himself prepared for the debates, from which the following three paragraphs are quoted:

Mr. Madison's own evidence.

The curiosity I had felt during my researches into the History of the most distinguished Confederacies, particularly those of antiquity, and the deficiency I found in the means of satisfying it more especially in what related to the process, the principles—the reasons, & the anticipations, which prevailed in the formation of them, determined me to preserve as far as I could an exact account of what might pass in the Convention whilst executing its trust, with the magnitude of which I was duly impressed, as I was with the gratification promised to future curiosity by an authentic exhibition of the objects, the opinions & the reasonings from which the new System of Govt. was to receive its peculiar structure & organization. Nor was I unaware of the value of such a contribution to the fund of materials for the History of a Constitution on which would be staked the happiness of a young people great even in its infancy, and possibly the cause of Liberty throught the world.

In pursuance of the task I had assumed I chose a seat in front of the presiding member, with the other members, on my right & left hand. In this favorable position for hearing all that passed, I noted in terms legible & in abbreviations & marks intelligible to myself what was read from the Chair or spoken by the members; and losing not a moment unnecessarily between the adjournment & reassembling of the Convention I was enabled to write out my daily notes during the session or within a few finishing days after its close, in the extent and form preserved in my own hand on my files.

In the labor and correctness of this I was not a little aided by practice, and by a familiarity with the style and the train of observation and reasoning which characterized the principal speakers. It happened, also, that I was not absent a single day, nor more than a casual fraction of an hour in any day, so that I could not have lost a single speech, unless a very short one.[1]

Nobly did Madison perform his mission, although the labor involved would have broken down the resolution of a more ordinary person. But, fortunately, James Madison was a determined little man, set in his ways, full of devotion to the cause in which his heart was enlisted and his nation involved, and permeated with an enthusiasm not sporadic only, but real and enduring. He found the duty, for duty it was, irksome. In a letter to his friend Thomas Jefferson, of July 18, 1787, when the conference was in the throes of the struggle between the pretensions of the big and the claims of the little States, in which Mr. Madison, as a delegate from Virginia, stood by the big States, he wrote:

His infinite patience and accuracy.

I have taken lengthy notes of everything that has yet passed, and mean to go on with the drudgery, if no indisposition obliges me to discontinue it.[2]

And he is reported to have remarked to his friend, Edward Coles, an early and highly respected governor of Illinois, " that the labor of writing out the debates, added to the confinement to which his attendance in Convention subjected him, almost killed him: but having under-

[1] *Documentary History of the Constitution*, vol. iii., pp. 796n-o; Hunt, *Writings of James Madison*, vol. ii., p. 410; Farrand, *Records of the Federal Convention*, vol. iii., p. 550.
[2] *Documentary History of the Constitution*, vol. iv., p. 236.

taken the task, he was determined to accomplish it."[1]

Mr. Jefferson in his turn, after reading and pondering the Notes, wrote under date of August 10, 1815, to John Adams, and during Mr. Madison's term as president of the United States:

Do you know that there exists in manuscript the ablest work of this kind ever yet executed, of the debates of the constitutional convention of Philadelphia in 1788 [87]? The whole of everything said and done there was taken down by Mr. Madison, with a labor and exactness beyond comprehension.[2]

If John Adams did not know, he doubtless suspected it, as the members of the conference looked upon Mr. Madison as its reporter even if he himself thought it best to have the Notes appear posthumously. In any event, Mr. Jefferson's statement as to Mr. Madison's labors and the accuracy of his manuscript is correct, for as a reporter he spared no efforts to attain accuracy during the Convention, and after its adjournment he took pains to fill up the few omissions which he noted upon reflection or rereading. Thus in a letter dated New York, August 21, 1789, although busied with the organization of the government under the Constitution, he nevertheless snatched a moment from his congressional duties to dragoon Edmund Randolph, soon to be

[1] Hugh Blair Grigsby, *The History of the Virginia Federal Convention of 1788*, 2 vols., vol. i., p. 95, note.

[2] Paul Leicester Ford, *The Writings of Thomas Jefferson*, vol. ix., p. 528.

the first Attorney General of the United States, who had introduced on behalf of his colleagues the Virginia plan, into furnishing him the notes of his address on that occasion, saying:

I find in looking over the notes of your introductory discourse in the Convention at Philada. that it is not possible for me to do justice to the substance of it. I am anxious for particular reasons to be furnished with the means of preserving this as well as the other arguments in that body, and must beg that you will make out & forward me the scope of your reasoning. You have your notes I know & from these you can easily deduce the argument on a condensed plan. I make this request with an earnestness wch. will not permit you either to refuse or delay a compliance.[1]

Mr. Randolph complied, and an abstract of the speech in his own handwriting is accordingly included in the Notes. But we know that this

[1] *Documentary History of the Constitution,* vol. v., p. 192.
Regarding the Virginian plan, often referred to as Mr. Randolph's, because he introduced it on behalf of the Virginian delegation, Mr. Madison says in the proposed preface to his Notes:
"On the arrival of the Virginian Deputies at Philadᵃ it occurred to them that from the early and prominent part taken by that State in bringing about the Convention some initiative step might be expected from them. The Resolutions introduced by Governor Randolph were the result of a Consultation on the subject; with an understanding that they left all the Deputies entirely open to the lights of discussion, and free to concur in any alterations or modifications which their reflections and judgements might approve. The Resolutions as the Journals shew became the basis on which the proceedings of the Convention commenced, and to the developments, variations and modifications of which the plan of Govᵗ proposed by the Convention may be traced." (*Documentary History of the Constitution,* vol. iii., 796m-n.)

help from the outside was rare, for Mr. Madison himself says in his draft of a preface,

With a very few exceptions the speeches were neither furnished, nor revised, nor sanctioned, by the speakers, but written out from my notes, aided by the freshness of my recollections . . . the exceptions alluded to were,—first, the sketch furnished by Mr. Randolph of his speech on the introduction of his propositions, on the twenty-ninth day of May; secondly the speech of Mr. Hamilton, who happened to call on me when putting the last hand to it, and who acknowledged its fidelity, without suggesting more than a very few verbal alterations which were made; thirdly, the speech of Gouverneur Morris on the second day of May [July], which was communicated to him on a like occasion, and who acquiesced in it without even a verbal change. The correctness of his language and the distinctness of his enunciation were particularly favorable to a reporter. The speeches of Doctor Franklin, excepting a few brief ones, were copied from the written ones read to the Convention by his colleague, Mr. Wilson, it being inconvenient to the Doctor to remain long on his feet.[1]

Indeed, Mr. Madison's conception of accuracy and of the reporter's duty was such as to cause him to preserve even the little " nasty " things said about himself, within and without the Convention. Thus in the session of July 5th, Mr. Patterson, sponsor of the New Jersey or small State plan, acknowledged that " the warmth [of

[1] Hunt, *Writings of James Madison*, vol. ii., p. 411; Farrand, *Records of the Federal Convention*, vol. iii., pp. 550-551.

Mr. Bedford] complained of was improper; but he thought the Sword & the Gallows little calculated to produce conviction. He complained of the manner in which Mʳ M— & Mʳ Govʳ Morris had treated the small States."[1] It would have been so easy to omit the last sentence altogether, or to leave only the reference to " Mr. Govr. Morris," who had been the chief offender. But this would not have been history, and the " Mr. *M,*" here referred to, was dealing with history. Again, it was only a very honest man, with a scrupulous, indeed one might say, an abnormal or extravagant regard for accuracy, who would record, preserve and add as a note to the session of June 15th, the following remarks made to him in person by John Dickinson:

You see the consequence of pushing things too far. Some of the members from the small States wish for two branches in the General Legislature, and are friends to a good National Government; but we would sooner submit to a foreign power, than submit to be deprived of an equality of suffrage, in both branches of the legislature, and thereby be thrown under the domination of the large States.[2]

Another instance of Madison's accuracy is the note appended to Charles Pinckney's speech in the session of June 25th, for which that young and aggressive but able person had carefully prepared himself, and which he wished to have handed

[1] *Documentary History of the Constitution,* vol. iii., p. 278.
[2] *Documentary History of the Constitution,* vol. iii., pp. 124-125.

down to posterity. The reporter included in his text the copy handed him, saying in a note, " the residue of this speech was not furnished like the above by Mr. Pinckney."[1] This otherwise trifling incident is important in that Pinckney's draft shows the accuracy of Mr. Madison's transcription.

A careful examination of the somewhat elaborate notes made by Robert Yates, a delegate from the State of New York, who, on July 10th, withdrew from the Convention in disgust at the way things were going; of the fragmentary and imperfect notes by Rufus King first published in 1894, Mr. King being a delegate from the State of Massachusetts, but later a distinguished resident of New York, and of the desultory and scattered notes which have more recently come to light of James McHenry, a delegate from the State of Maryland, only establishes Mr. Madison's accuracy, sets his skill as a reporter *hors de concours,* and confirms to the letter Mr. Jefferson's opinion " that the whole of everything said and done there was taken down by Mr. Madison with a labor and exactness beyond comprehension."

[1] *Documentary History of the Constitution,* vol. iii., p. 207.

ORIGIN OF THE CONFERENCE

The condition of affairs in America on the eve of the conference filled many an observer abroad with dismay and many a citizen at home with apprehension lest the fair fruits of the Revolution be lost, lest for example out of the erstwhile colonies, held more or less in check by the mother country, now States united but not harmonious under the Articles of Confederation, there might emerge thirteen sovereign, free and independent States bent upon exercising their sovereignty, freedom and independence after the manner of their elders if not betters of Europe. There was a profound and general dread in America of any form of government under which the interest of the one might prevail over that of the many, and the common good be sacrificed to the ambition of the few strong enough to satisfy their political ambitions and predatory appetites. How to make their world "safe for democracy" was as keen a question then as for us now.

The prevailing anxiety.

In the unfinished preface to the Notes written some forty years later, Mr. Madison briefly touched upon the situation, which, indeed, he had treated more fully in his Memorandum on the defects of the Confederation. In the closing days of his life, certain conditions, even those ceasing to exist long ago, stood out undimmed by age and so important that they could neither be overlooked in retrospection nor left unrecorded by this most conscientious of observers. In respect to the relations of the States with one another and with foreign Powers, he then felt justified in saying:

At the date of the Convention, the aspect & retrospect of the pol. condition of the U. S. could

Specific difficulties. not but fill the pub. mind with a gloom which was relieved only by a hope that so select a Body would devise an adequate remedy for the existing and prospective evils so impressively demanding it.

It was seen that the public debt rendered so sacred by the cause in which it had been incurred remained without any provision for its payment. The reiterated and elaborate efforts of Cong. to procure from the States a more adequate power to raise the means of payment had failed. The effect of the ordinary requisitions of Congress had only displayed the inefficiency of the authy. making them; none of the States having duly complied with them, some having failed altogether or nearly so; . . .

The want of authy. in Congs. to regulate Commerce had produced in Foreign nations particularly G. B. a monopolizing policy injurious to the trade of the U. S. and destructive to their navigation; . . .

The same want of a general power over Commerce led to an exercise of this power separately, by the States, wch. not only proved abortive, but engendered rival, conflicting and angry regulations. Besides the vain attempts to supply their respective treasuries by imposts, which turned their commerce into the neighboring   ports,

. . . the States having ports for foreign commerce, taxed & irritated the adjoining States,
trading thro' them, as N. Y. Pena. Virga. & S.
Carolina. Some of the States, as Connecticut,
taxed imports as from Massts. higher than imports even from G. B. of wch. Massts. complained to Virga. and doubtless to other States.

. . .

In certain cases the Fedl. authy. was violated
by Treaties & wars with Indians, as by Geo.:
by troops, raised & kept up, witht. the consent of
Congs. as by Massts. by compacts witht. the consent of Congs. as between Pena. and N. Jersey,
and between Virga. and Maryd.[1]

But these matters relate primarily to their
outward conduct. " In the internal administration of the States," Mr. Madison continued, " a
violations of Contracts had become familiar in
the form of depreciated paper made a legal
tender, of property substituted for money, of In-
stalment laws, and of the occlusions of the Courts
of Justice; although evident that all such inter-
ferences affected the rights of other States, rela-
tively Creditor, as well as Citizens Creditors
within the States." [2]
And after enumerating instances of lack of uniformity " in cases requiring it," such as naturalization, bankruptcy laws, and the want of " a
coercive authority operating on individuals and
a guaranty of the internal tranquillity of the
States," he drew the natural consequence from

[1] *Documentary History of the Constitution*, vol. iii., pp. 796*i-j.*
[2] *Documentary History of the Constitution*, vol. iii., p. 796*k.*

this condition of the Union that " the Fedl. authy. had ceased to be respected abroad, and dispositions shewn there, particularly in G. B., to take advantage of its imbecility, and to speculate on its approaching downfall; at home it had lost all confidence & credit. The unstable and unjust career of the States had also forfeited the respect & confidence essential to order and good Govt., involving a general decay of confidence & credit between man & man." [1]

In a word the States had patched up a union during the war of independence in order to obtain its recognition by Great Britain; and with the signing of the treaty of peace on September 3, 1783, between that country and representatives of the United States, mentioning each of the thirteen by name, and recognizing them " to be free, sovereign and independent States," to quote from the Treaty, the politicians of the day apparently lost interest in the Union which had served its purpose, and turned their undivided attention to domestic affairs of their respective States. If, however, the States were to live together, and geography had done its best to settle that question for them, they either had to observe the Articles of Confederation, revising them where faulty or inadequate, or, brushing the Articles aside, to settle by treaty the relations that they should sustain with one another.

Alternatives.

The regulation of commerce which had caused the colonies to turn their backs upon the mother

[1] *Documentary History of the Constitution,* vol. iii., p. 796k.

country, was destined to draw the States together. The State of Maryland owned the Potomac River and claimed jurisdiction to low water mark on the Virginian shore. This was a source of contention on the part of the larger commonwealth, but the Maryland charter was clear, or at least so clear that the Virginian men of affairs, lawyers as well as laymen, could not successfully contest the claim. Both States were deeply interested in Chesapeake Bay, into which the Potomac empties, and which extends far into Maryland and discharges its waters through Virginia into the Atlantic Ocean. Then, too, Pennsylvania, adjoining Maryland on the north and almost touching the bay into which the Susquehanna River flows, and Delaware, to the east of Maryland, were interested in any regulation of commerce upon the bay and its tributaries. These familiar facts are but a few of the long array of commercial difficulties destined to influence the course of our national growth. *The regulation of commerce.*

The immediate result was that in 1785 a meeting at Alexandria in Virginia, of delegates from Maryland and Virginia, artfully entertained at Mount Vernon by the great Washington, led to the suggestion that the States generally should be invited to consider in common the regulation of navigation and commerce in their common interest. *Meeting at Alexandria.*

In May of the same year the legislature of Massachusetts, upon the recommendation of Governor Bowdoin, passed a resolution declaring inade-

quate the Articles of Confederation and calling
for a Convention from all the States. But the
resolution never reached the Congress.

In the early days of 1786, the legislature of
Virginia therefore appointed commissioners, of
whom Mr. Madison was one, to consider how far
a uniform system of interstate commercial regulations was "necessary to their common interest
and their permanent harmony," directing them
to invite the several States to send delegates to a
convention for that purpose. The first Monday
of September was agreed upon as the time, and
the little town of Annapolis, then and now the
capital of Maryland, as the place of meeting.

At
Annapolis.

Nine accepted the invitation and appointed
delegates, but only the representatives of five of
the States appeared. Under these circumstances
it did not seem worth while for a part to devise
regulations for the whole. The delegates therefore wisely contented themselves with a report
of the meeting to the States, signed by John Dickinson as chairman, but drafted by the deft hand
of Alexander Hamilton.[1] They sent a copy to
the Congress for its information and action, and
recommended the appointment of delegates of
the States to meet in Philadelphia, on the second
Monday in May of the ensuing year, in order
to revise the articles of Confederation. Virginia
put itself in touch with the States, urging them
to comply with the recommendation.

The Congress ultimately approved the plan, in-

[1] *Documentary History of the Constitution,* vol. i., pp. 1-5.

fluenced, no doubt, by acts of rebellion in Massachusetts against the government of that State and by the fear of similar outbreaks in other States; and the Convention was officially called by the Congress, as stated in its resolution of February 21, 1787, for

the sole and express purpose of revising the Articles of Confederation, and reporting to the Congress and the several legislatures, such alterations and provisions therein, as shall, when agreed to in Congress, and confirmed by the States, render the Federal Constitution adequate to the exigencies of Government, and the preservation of the Union.[1]

Call of the Convention.

All of the thirteen States, with the exception of the pigmy commonwealth of Rhode Island and Providence Plantations, appointed delegates to meet at the time and the place fixed for the meeting, and, as the world knows, the Articles of Confederation were revised with a vengeance by throwing them overboard the Ship of State and by drafting a scheme of government adequate to the needs of the States, because based upon their experience both as colonies and as States.

ACCOMPLISHING THE IMPOSSIBLE

The second Monday of May, 1787, fell upon the 14th, but on that day only two delegations appeared at Philadelphia, the Pennsylvanian, which could not well fail to be on hand, and the Vir-

[1] *Documentary History of the Constitution*, vol. i., p. 8.

The impossible task. ginian group with the punctual Washington at its head. It was not until Friday, the 25th of the month, when the delegates of seven States, that is, a majority of the thirteen then forming the Union, appeared and convened in the very city and stately building where eleven years previously the Declaration of Independence had been approved, proclaimed, and signed. The place and the hour were big with possibilities for the future. What was to take place? Chastened by the experience of eleven years of anxiety and apprehension, what would the conference bring forth? Could the States possibly create and maintain a more perfect union based upon the separation of the powers of both, and upon the recognition of the interdependence of each? It seemed impossible. Nevertheless the fifty-five delegates to the Convention, of which Thomas Jefferson said with pardonable exaggeration, " it is really an assembly of demigods "[1]—accomplished the impossible by good will, concession, and compromise. And yet, three of the members present at the signing of the Constitution, Messrs. Mason and Randolph of Virginia, and Mr. Gerry of Massachusetts, refused to add their names to those of their thirty-nine colleagues, although that document owed very much to their labors.

This Federal Convention was, as already stated, an international conference, and as such it would

---

[1] Letter of Thomas Jefferson, dated Paris, Aug. 30, 1787, addressed to John Adams. (*Documentary History of the Constitution,* vol. iv., p. 266.)

have been opened in person by the venerable Benjamin Franklin, then President of the commonwealth of Pennsylvania, who "alone could have
been thought of as a competitor" and who would
have proposed George Washington, of Virginia,
as its President, had not, as Mr. Madison informs
us, "the state of the weather and of his health
confined" the illustrious Pennsylvanian "to his
house."[1] As it was, Robert Morris, senior member of the Pennsylvanian delegation, in his absence, made the motion, seconded by John Rutledge of South Carolina, and, upon ballot taken,
General Washington was found to be unanimously
elected, as he had been chosen Commander in
Chief of the Revolutionary Army by the Congress, and as he was twice later, and because of President
the Convention, to be elected President of the Secretary.
United States. After a few words from the
newly elected President, modestly disclaiming
merit on his part, as was his wont, and as
appears to be also the custom in international
conferences, Mr. Wilson, next in rank in the
Pennsylvanian delegation, rose and proposed for
Secretary, William Temple Franklin, grandson of
the great doctor; then "Colonel," as Mr. Madison calls him, but Alexander Hamilton as we of
today would say, proposed a companion in arms,
one Major William Jackson. A ballot was taken,
the States divided five to two against the grandson, and the Major was declared elected—a bad
choice, be it said, with due deference to the

[1] *Documentary History of the Constitution,* vol. iii., p. 9.

Colonel, his sponsor, and the five States that voted for him. For if we are to judge by the Major's journal, as we must in the absence of the notes of the proceedings which he claims to have taken, but which, mislaid or lost, have disappeared without a trace of their existence, the official Secretary's services left not a little to be desired.

Creden-
tials.

The Convention now had an efficient President and a titular Secretary. The credentials of the

Commit-
tee on
rules and
orders.

delegates of the several States and the instructions contained in them, were read, whereupon the Convention was organized and in session. Other details were promptly arranged. A committee was appointed " to prepare standing rules and orders," and the Convention adjourned from Friday, the 25th, until Monday, the 28th, to allow the committee to meet and prepare its report. At the session of the 28th the committee reported and, with an amendment and an addition, the rules were adopted by virtue whereof each State had, as under the Articles of Confederation, one vote

Vote by
States.

irrespective of the number of the delegates, and the votes of the States were recorded, not the names of the delegates casting them. " A house to do business," to quote Mr. Madison's language, consisted " of the deputies of not less than seven States "; all questions were to " be decided by the greater number of these which shall be fully represented," but a smaller number could adjourn from day to day.[1]

[1] *Documentary History of the Constitution,* vol. iii., p. 11.

Committees were to be elected by ballot, and they were not to sit while the Convention was in session, as the attendance of all at the general meetings was deemed desirable. It was further provided that nothing spoken was to be printed or otherwise published or communicated without leave. Such were the main features of the Convention's organization.

Election of committees by ballot.

These are, it will be observed, the methods of an international conference, with the differences only that nominations were to be made and decided by ballot, not by a silence that is held to betoken assent, and that resolutions or proposals were to be adopted by a majority instead of by the unanimous vote of all the States. But it is not unreasonable to believe that future international conferences may, both as to election by ballot and to adoption by majority, profit by the experience of the Federal Convention, which is to date the only international conference whose labors have stood the test of time and of criticism. This seems probable because self-respecting States can not be expected to have the larger States organize the conference by prearrangement without consulting the delegates of the less powerful nations, and because it may prove undesirable to continue the unanimity rule when no State is bound by its vote in conference or even by the vote of the conference except as the state signifies its own ratification after formal submission of the project for separate approval or disapproval. But the point to be borne in mind

Significance for Society of Nations.

—a theme to which reference will frequently be made—is that the Federal Convention of 1787 is an abiding object lesson for the student of international conferences.

GENERAL INTERESTS

The Articles of Confederation provided for a Union of the States, with a Congress as its legislative and executive organs, so far as the States divested themselves of and granted legislative functions to the United States. No judiciary, as such, was created, although the Congress of the Confederation was vested with the power of "appointing courts for the trial of piracies and felonies committed on the high seas and establishing courts for receiving and determining finally appeals in all cases of captures," with the power of appointing temporary tribunals or commissions " in all disputes and differences now subsisting or that hereafter may arise between two or more States concerning boundary jurisdiction or any other cause whatever," including " all controversies concerning the private right of soil claimed under different grants of two or more States."[1] How should the conference readapt the judiciary to the new needs of the new day?

But there were other and not less serious difficulties. In the Continental Congress each State could be represented by not less than two, nor more than seven delegates, subject to recall, and

The more serious problems presented by the Articles of Confederation.

[1] Articles of Confederation, Article IX.

who were to receive such compensation for their services as their States might be pleased to allow. But, irrespective of the number of delegates, each State was to have, and actually did have only one vote in the Congress, a provision galling upon the large States, but the price of confederation, as it was to be the price of the more perfect union of the Constitution. The Articles, as a purely diplomatic document, acted upon the States, not upon their citizens, and could only be changed or amended by unanimous consent. Less important measures required the vote of nine States, and during the recess of the Congress a committee of the States sat to conduct affairs, with power to transact such business as nine States might authorize, but not to do anything " for the exercise of which, by the articles of confederation, the voice of nine States in the Congress of the United States assembled is requisite." [1]

But still more serious in the exercise of the powers specifically granted to the United States in Congress assembled, of which the States had divested themselves, the Congress could only *recommend* as it had no way of *compelling* the States to comply. It could not disregard the State and lay its hand upon the citizen, as in a national form of government. The Congress was authorized to enter into treaties with foreign countries, the States renouncing in behalf of " the firm league of friendship with each other " [2] the

Impotence of the central authority.

---

[1] Articles of Confederation, Article X.
[2] Articles of Confederation, Article III.

exercise of this right, possessed by them as sovereign, free and independent States,[1] but the Congress could not enforce the observance of the treaties; the States renounced the right to form treaties, alliances or agreements between themselves, but if they did the Congress was helpless to undo them; the Congress could determine the quota of troops to be furnished by each State which might or might not comply, without any power on the part of the Congress other than of persuasion arising from the needs of the occasion. The Congress could determine the amount of revenue to be raised for general purposes to be " supplied by the several States, in proportion to the value of all land within each State, granted to or surveyed for any person, as such land and the buildings and improvements thereon "; but, as the taxes for paying the proportions thus determined were to " be laid and levied by the authority and direction of the Legislatures of the several States," it is evident that the revenue of the United States would, in last resort, depend upon the pleasure of the several States.[2] Attempts to change the basis of liability for quotas or taxes from the value of land to the number of inhabitants or citizens, to raise a revenue by duties upon imports, and to regulate commerce between and among the States, failed because of the inability in each case to obtain the unanimous consent of the several States.

[1] Articles of Confederation, Article II.
[2] Articles of Confederation, Article VIII.

Without pursuing the subject further it is obvious that the conference must endeavor to grant to the general government the means to make its limited powers effective within the terms of the grants. The more perfect union would thus be empowered to raise the revenue needed to carry on the business of government, to regulate navigation and commerce. Besides, means must be devised either for coercing the States, or for allowing the general government to reach the citizens of the States directly, without the intervention or agency of the State. In other words, some method for dealing to the extent of its authority with citizens bound by law and subject to suit, instead of with States making law but immune from process, was necessary for the central government. The only other recourse would be war which, as Mr. Madison justly said, would abrogate the treaty, compact or agreement. It was further obvious that in framing a new government for such of the several States as might be minded to ratify it, the delegates would naturally draw upon the experience which the States had had in constitution-making before and since the Declaration of Independence. The government of the perfected union would probably consist of a legislature, of an executive and of a judiciary, authorized to exercise the powers to the extent of the constitutional grant but not beyond. This was particularly likely because of the threefold division of power as embodied in the Virginian Bill of Rights, antedating the

Obvious reforms needed.

Declaration of Independence and followed by the other States, and also because the movement to amend the Articles of Confederation came from Virginia. Furthermore, Virginia's great citizen was president of the Convention and its delegation was the most influential delegation on the floor of the "House". It was also to be expected that the judiciary would play a conspicuous rôle in any scheme of government which the delegates might devise, for without a central judiciary every treaty might conceivably receive thirteen different interpretations, as the treaty was the law of each of the States and subject as such to interpretation by the court of each State. Separate coordinate State courts might present the spectacle of any one act of the general legislature, binding the State and its citizens, being interpreted and applied in thirteen different ways.

Again it was certain that the States styled "sovereign, free and independent" in the Articles of Confederation would only consent to the renunciation of specified, enumerated powers of a general nature, belonging more appropriately to the general government than to any State. Such a limited renunciation in the common interest of the several States, rather than in the interest of any one or of any group thereof, seemed necessary. But it was apparent throughout that they intended to reserve or retain for themselves all powers which they did not consent to grant to the government of the Union. Further it was to be anticipated that the Constitution would be subject to amendment, as experience had shown the necessity of amending the Articles, and that the Amendments, not too easily adopted, would yet be made by less than the unanimous vote of the States. And, finally, it must have been foreseen that the struggle begun in Congress between the large and the small States, the small claiming equality of right with the large, would make its appearance in the Convention, and that the States or sections would stand out for their special or sectional interests; that navigation and commerce in the eastern carrying and trading States, and that the slave trade and property in slaves in the Southern States for example, would all demand attention. In other words, it was in the nature of things that the Constitution, if drafted, would have to be a creature of concessions in the relations of the large and the small, and of compromise in the matter of local or sectional interests of the peoples of the States.

But before taking up the proceedings of the conference on these various matters, it is well to premise that, on the very day on which the conference resolved itself into a Committee of the Whole, May 30, 1787, the day after Mr. Randolph had "opened the main business" with his address on behalf of the Virginian delegation and in justification of its plan, the delegates made The bold decision. the bold decision of postponing the proposition to amend the Articles of Confederation by adopting the motion "that a *national* Government ought to be established, consisting of a supreme legislative, executive & judiciary." In the light of the resolution adopted by the Congress limiting the Convention to a revision of the Articles of Confederation, and in view of the instructions of the several States to their respective delegates to the same effect, this was indeed a decision bold as it was momentous. It is easy to justify this act of the Convention from the technical point of view, in that its draft of a Constitution was, in form and in effect, merely a recommendation to the States, to be accepted or rejected by them in the exercise of their sovereign discretion; but perhaps the best justification is that of President Washington, who remarked: " If to please the people, we offer what we ourselves disapprove, how can we afterward defend our work? " [1]

This action of the Convention could only mean that the Union of the States was indeed to have a government adequate to its needs. It should be said, however, in this connection, that, in the course of subsequent proceedings, the word " national " was unanimously struck from the phrase " national government" on the motion of Mr. Ellsworth of Connecticut that the government to be established should be not a national government, as originally proposed by Mr. Randolph and approved by the partizans of what was then called consolidation, but " a government of the United States," to consist of the threefold divi-

---

[1] Gouverneur Morris, *An oration upon the Death of General Washington* p. 21; delivered in New York, December 31, 1799 (Farrand, *Records of the Federal Convention,* vol. iii., 382.)

sion, which, in Mr. Ellsworth's view and apparently in that of the Convention, was the proper title. But by the terms of the resolution adopted by the conference at the first session of the Committee of the Whole, it was apparent that the delegates proposed to ignore their " instructions " and to " revise " the Articles of Confederation by supplanting them.

The matter of the equality of States came up before the opening of the Convention and was only got out of the way by concession from both sides in July. The questions involving local interests were settled only in the closing days of the conference. These two sets of difficulties, seemingly insurmountable then, are still peculiarly significant to international conferences. Agreement on all other matters, essential to the organization of the government of the Union, was found to be comparatively easy on the principle of give and take, a principle which is also the very life and breath of any international conference. The two issues, equality and local interests, were so acute that they will be considered in some detail before proceeding to an analysis and appreciation of the international document which we call the Constitution.

Mr. Madison tells us somewhat casually, and in a note of later date which he appended to the completed manuscript of the Session of May 28th, that " previous to the arrival of a majority of the States, the rule by which they ought to vote in the Convention had been made a subject

Equality of States.

of conversation among the members present ".[1]
Gouverneur Morris, Robert Morris, and others
from Pennsylvania—Massachusetts, Pennsylvania, and Virginia were then the large
States—were of the opinion that they should
unite in denying an equal vote " as unreasonable, and as enabling the small States to
negative every good system of Government," proposed, of course, by the large for the benefit of
the small States, " which must in the nature of
things," according to the views of the large States,

Large
and
small
States.

" be founded on a violation of that equality."
Mr. Madison was strongly in favor of the equal
rights of the great States, as delegates of great
States usually are, and believed, no doubt hon-
estly, that the claim of the small States to an
equality of vote was preposterous, much as Bishop
Horsley was pleased to assert that the only interest the people had in laws was " to obey them." [2]
But he recalled the inability of the Continental
Congress to adopt any other principle than that
of equality in the matter of representation in the
very Articles which the conference was called to
amend.

At least Messrs. Washington and Madison, of
the Virginian delegation, were practical, hard-
headed men, and they were set upon getting the
most effective general government to be had,

[1] *Documentary History of the Constitution,* vol. iii., p. 10, footnote.
[2] " Dr. Horsley, Bishop of Rochester, ' did not know what the
mass of the people in any country had to do with the laws, but to
obey them.' " (Sir Thomas Erskine May, *Constitutional History of
England,* Holland's edition, 1912, vol. ii., p. 55.)

without breaking up the Convention at the out-
set. They apparently possessed the hope that
intimate association with the delegates of the
larger States would impress the other delegates
with their superior wisdom and reasonableness.
However that may be, "the members from Virginia," Mr. Madison says, "conceiving that such
an attempt might beget fatal altercations between
the large & small States, and that it would be
easier to prevail on the latter, in the course of the
deliberations, to give up their equality for the
sake of an effective Government, than on taking the field of discussion, to disarm themselves
of the right & thereby throw themselves on the
mercy of the large States, discountenanced &
stifled the project."[1]

The Virginian plan of taking the little ones
in hand and bringing them to reason did not and
could not work, as the small States, like the large,
were only willing to renounce a right in the interest of the whole, not in the interest of any group
other than their own, and then only when the
renunciation seemed to them "safe," of which
each of the States was to judge.

The basis
for renun-
ciation.

This was very bluntly expressed during the grill-
ing process to which the small were put by the
large States, which could neither be considered
their elders nor their betters, and it is recorded by
Mr. Madison, whose honesty as a reporter, be it
again said, is even more astonishing than his skill,
in the summary of his long and comprehensive

[1] *Documentary History of the Constitution*, vol. iii., p. 10, footnote.

address in the session of June 19th, which he no doubt hoped would " prevail " upon the small States, " in the course of the deliberations, to give up their equality for the sake of an effective Government." Mr. Madison, as reported in his Notes, said that " the great difficulty lies in the affair of Representation; and if this could be adjusted, all others would be surmountable." [1] Nothing could be truer, as the event amply demonstrated. Mr. Madison then continued: " It was admitted by both the gentlemen from N. Jersey [Mr. Brearly and Mr. Paterson] that it would not *be just to allow Virga.* which was 16 times as large as Delaware an equal vote only." [2]

" Safe."   In the abstract they may have been right, but the admission did not show any marked conversion to the " reasonable " point of view of the large States, inasmuch as, according to Mr. Madison, " their language was that it would not be *safe for Delaware* to allow Virg.ª 16 times as many votes." [3]

That was the crux of the question and the solution was brutally stated by Mr. or General Pinckney, for there were two delegates of that name from South Carolina, when, in the session of June 6th, one or the other of them said—Mr. Madison ascribing the remark to the Mister, Mr. Yates to the General—: " The whole comes to this . . . Give N. Jersey an equal vote, and she will

---

[1] *Documentary History of the Constitution,* vol. iii., p. 160.
[2] *Documentary History of the Constitution,* vol. iii., p. 161.
[3] *Documentary History of the Constitution,* vol. iii., p. 161.

dismiss her scruples, and concur in the Nat! system." [1]

The Convention having come to a standstill— "We are now at a full stop," to use the homely but expressive language of Mr. Sherman [2] of Connecticut—and in response to a general feeling that "Something must be done, or we shall disappoint not only America, but the whole world," to quote Mr. Gerry [3] of Massachusetts, the great and good General Pinckney proposed, at the very same session of July 2d, in which these remarks had been made, but before they were uttered, that "a Committee . . . be appointed to devise & report some compromise," to consist of a member from each of the eleven States represented, as two of the three delegates from New York had withdrawn, and the delegates from New Hampshire, although appointed, had not yet arrived. [4]

There was a way out, and it was found not by any one, but by the collective wisdom of the conference, as so often happens. To Mr. Madison and to many the question seemed to be as he had put it in the session of June 20th:

Committee on "Compromise."

---

[1] *Documentary History of the Constitution*, vol. iii., p. 136.

It is immaterial whether Mr. Pinckney or Mr. C. C. Pinckney—that is to say, the General—made the above remark, and it is only noted in passing as showing Mr. Madison's accuracy in substance, if not always in form. Thus Robert Yates, a delegate from New York, recounts the incident: "Mr. C. C. Pinckney supposes that if N-Jersey was indulged with one vote out of 13, she would have no objection to a national government." (*Secret Proceedings and Debates of the Federal Convention*, p. 127, published in 1821.)

[2] *Documentary History of the Constitution*, vol. iii., p. 264.

[3] *Documentary History of the Constitution*, vol. iii., p. 269.

[4] *Documentary History of the Constitution*, vol. iii., p. 264.

In a word; the two extremes before us are a perfect separation & a perfect incorporation, of the 13 States. In the first case they would be independent nations subject to no law, but the law of nations. In the last, they would be mere counties of one entire republic, subject to one common law. [1]

The two extremes.

In fact, the compromise was very simple. As the legislature was to consist of two branches the small States conceded representation proportioned to the population of each State in the lower branch of the legislature, called therefore the House of Representatives; the larger States conceded equality of representation in the upper house, called the Senate, in which each State should be represented by two members chosen by the legislatures of each of the several States. In the lower house, each State was to have a member for each 40,000, later reduced to 30,000, inhabitants. In the upper house, the members were to vote individually, each casting a vote, not one casting the two votes of the State, a device apparently adopted to secure a vote for the purpose of a quorum when one or other of the members of a State might be absent. In addition, revenue bills were to originate in the lower house, to be accepted or rejected in the upper house, a provision ultimately modified so as to permit the Senate to amend but not originate bills of this nature. Inasmuch as a bill to become a law had to pass both houses, the origin of the bill,

The compromise on Representation.

---

[1] *Documentary History of the Constitution*, vol. iii., p. 232.

which can be amended in either house out of all resemblance to its former self, was a matter of no great consequence and was so regarded by the larger States. The truth is the committee and the conference were at their wits' end to devise something that might seem to be a fair concession from each side, as the delegates of the big States were genuinely anxious to save their faces and the delegates of the little States were equally anxious to help them in the process.

They were set, however, on preserving the fruits of victory which they had literally snatched from the very jaws of defeat. And, curiously, it was Gouverneur Morris, who, on September 15th, the last business day of the Convention, as the session of the 17th was formal and restricted primarily to signing, moved to render forever impossible the inequality of the States under the Constitution of the United States. Again, it is the honest Mr. Madison who thus reports the incident, not unmixed perhaps with a touch of retrospective irony, in connection with Article V, concerning Amendments:

Mr. Gove^r Morris moved to annex a further proviso—" that no State, without its consent shall be deprived of its equal suffrage in the Senate." [1]

And the big State man had the best of reasons for his eleventh hour conversion to the views of the little States. " This motion," Mr. Madison

[1] *Documentary History of the Constitution,* vol. iii., p. 758.

continues, "being dictated by the circulating murmurs of the small States was agreed to without debate, no one opposing it, or on the question, saying no."[1]

LOCAL INTERESTS

The leading and far-sighted statesmen of Virginia were against the slave trade, the existence

Slaves. and extension of slavery, George Mason and Mr. Madison speaking eloquently against it. George Washington, as is well known, emancipated his slaves, and Thomas Jefferson never got over the omission from his draft of the Declaration of Independence of the denunciation of King George for fastening slavery upon the colonies.

The Northern States were not in favor of slavery. They would have preferred to see it wiped out, and the attitude of the Middle States was similar. The delegates of the Carolinas, North and South, and Georgia, however, were inexorable. They held that slaves were property and that they should be recognized as such.

At the same time the slave was to figure as a man in estimating population and in fixing the basis of representation in the Congress, in accordance with the resolution of the Continental Congress in the proportion of five slaves to three white men. But the delegates of the slave States were not so anxious to have their slaves counted

---

[1] *Documentary History of the Constitution*, vol. iii., p. 758.

for purposes of direct taxation, although they yielded the point.

The slave trade was to be allowed, or rather it was not to be prohibited, until 1808. The Southern States had already secured for their citizens the return of their fugitive slaves who should escape to a sister State in which slavery might not exist, and they made what they were pleased to consider a concession that a tax or duty not exceeding ten dollars might be laid upon each slave imported from the outside world. This, however, was not enough; the three States insisted upon their right to stock up with slaves before the slave trade could be stopped, and they further demanded that the right to do so be secured by a proviso that the Constitution could not be amended in that particular prior to 1808.

How did it happen that the will of the three prevailed against the judgment, or at least the preference, of the majority? In this way. The Eastern States insisted that Congress should have the power to pass laws affecting navigation and commerce by a mere majority, whereas the Southern farming States depending upon the exportation of their agricultural products and the importation of wares in return wished to require a majority of two-thirds, as in the case of treaties, for the validity of rules or regulations affecting navigation or commerce. The Eastern States were unwilling to confederate if the hands of Congress were tied in this matter and in this manner; the three Southern States were unwilling to confederate unless the slave trade were admitted and safeguarded. Politics, they say, make queer bedfellows. The Eastern and the three Southern States, willing to sacrifice the common good if need be for their special interests, joined forces with the result that the bargain, for such it was, passed without a dissenting vote in the matter of navigation. The bargain was, as will presently appear, that Congress might pass laws regulating navigation and commerce by a majority vote, and that the slave trade might go on for twenty years. The delegates of the Northern and Middle States saw in the acceptance of the scheme the price of union, and their grandchildren of the North and the South paid the price of union in the best blood and unspeakable treasure of both sections.

The history of the miserable compromise faithfully chronicled by Mr. Madison should make the good people of the North chary in criticism

The commercial motive.

of the good people of the South. Thus Mr. Gorham of Massachusetts, President of the Continental Congress, and Chairman of the Committee of the Whole, when the Convention met in this more informal manner, said in the session of August 22d: "He desired it to be remembered that the Eastern States had no motive to Union but a commercial one. They were able to protect themselves. They were not afraid of external danger, and did not need the aid of the Southern States."[1] Again, in the session of the

[1] *Documentary History of the Constitution*, vol. iii., p. 591.

29th of August, he recurred to the larger vote
to be required in legislation affecting navigation
and commerce, saying on this occasion:

If the Government is to be so fettered as to be
unable to relieve the Eastern States what motive
can they have to join in it, and thereby tie their
own hands from measures which they could otherwise take for themselves. The Eastern States
were not led to strengthen the Union by fear for
their own safety.[1]

On their side the delegates from the three Southern States did not prostrate themselves before their
brethren of the Northeast. In the session of August 22d, where Mr. Gorham had candidly avowed
that the Eastern " did not need the aid of the
Southern States," General Pinckney warned that
the delegates of South Carolina could not sign
the Constitution without adequate recognition and
protection of slavery, and that if they did, their
States would not ratify it, saying:

S. Carolina & Georgia cannot do without slaves.
As to Virginia she will gain by stopping the
importations. Her slaves will rise in value, &
she has more than she wants. It would be
unequal to require S. C. & Georgia to confederate
on such terms . . . He contended that the importation of slaves would be for the interest of the
whole Union. The more slaves, the more produce to employ the carrying trade; The more
consumption also, and the more of this, the more
of revenue for the common treasury. He admit-

[1] *Documentary History of the Constitution*, vol. iii., p. 641.

ted it to be reasonable that slaves should be dutied like other imports, but should consider a rejection of the clause as an exclusion of S. Carolina from the Union.[1]

Again a Compromise. The slave trade was therefore allowed, but in the first instance not to extend beyond the year 1800. In the session of August 25th the General moved to substitute 1808, thus prolonging the trade for eight years. And Mr. Gorham, whose mind was set on protecting the interest which his section had in navigation and commerce, just as General Pinckney was looking after the interests of his, "2 ded the motion" as reported by Mr. Madison, who followed Mr. Gorham with a statement in his own behalf that "Twenty years will produce all the mischief that can be apprehended from the liberty to import slaves."[2] Still the motion was carried: New Hampshire, Massachusetts, Connecticut, Maryland, and the three Southern States voting in its favor; New Jersey, Pennsylvania, Delaware, Virginia, voting against it, New York not being represented.[3]

In the session of August 29th, in which Mr. Gorham for the second time reminded the delegates that "the Eastern States were not led to strengthen the Union by fear for their own safety," General Pinckney, speaking as the plenipotentiary of three Southern States, and they could not have found an abler man, said:

[1] *Documentary History of the Constitution*, vol. iii., p. 587.
[2] *Documentary History of the Constitution*, vol. iii., p. 616.
[3] *Documentary History of the Constitution*, vol. iii., p. 616.

It was the true interest of the S. States to have no regulation of commerce; but considering the loss brought on the commerce of the Eastern States by the revolution, their liberal conduct toward the views of South Carolina, and the interest of the weak South[n] States, he thought it proper that no fetters should be imposed on the power of making commercial regulations; and that his constituents, though prejudiced against the Eastern States, would be reconciled to this liberality—He had himself, he said, prejudices ag[st] the Eastern States before he came here, but would acknowledge that he had found them as liberal and candid as any men whatever. [1]

As Mr. Madison expressed it in after years, in a note to this passage, " He [General Pinckney] meant the permission to import slaves. An understanding on the two subjects of *navigation* and *slavery,* had taken place between those parts of the Union, which explains the vote on the Motion depending, as well as the language of Genl. Pinckney & others." [2] When, therefore, the vote was taken to strike out the requirement of a two-thirds majority in navigation acts, it was agreed to as Mr. Madison says, " nem. con ".[3] Of a truth, a fellow interest as well as " a fellow feeling makes us wondrous kind."

These two incidents have been dwelt upon at considerable length to make it clear from the experience of the Federal Convention that while

[1] *Documentary History of the Constitution,* vol. iii., p. 637.
[2] *Documentary History of the Constitution,* vol. iii., p. 637, footnote.
[3] *Documentary History of the Constitution,* vol. iii., p. 642.

men of good will could not successfully compromise irreconcilable interests involving fundamental conceptions of right or wrong, yet they
could reach a "working agreement" by mutual
concession in a fundamental principle such as
equality, not involving, as we would say today,
moral turpitude.   There are some things that
majorities or unanimity can not do, as when Syd-
ney Smith wittily stumped the leader of the over-
whelming Tory majority in Parliament to take
advantage of its strength to repeal the Pytha-
gorean Theorem!   Within this line, the nations
of the Society of Nations can go as far as the
States of the American Union in conference
assembled, and Mr. Madison's Notes will show
them how honest men, when not confronted by
wholly irreconcilable interests, such as black and
white, can "safely" afford to act.

LEGISLATURE, EXECUTIVE, JUDICIARY

These two great questions out of the way, the
conference reached without serious difficulty a
workable agreement, as events have proved, upon
the legislative department with an upper and a
lower branch, upon specific matters concerning
the States as a whole, and upon laws binding the
United States, the States, and peoples within each
of them.

Powers to be granted to an executive called the
President, were agreed upon, such as the power
to execute the laws of the more perfect union.   It

was easily agreed that he should be elected for a period of years, the number of years giving rise to much controversy. It was also agreed that he be eligible to reelection by the people within the States, responsible to them for the faithful performance of the rights and duties of his office, subject to impeachment in the Senate representing the States at the instance of the House of Representatives, and removable upon trial under the presidency of the Chief Justice of the Supreme Court, if convicted by a two-thirds vote of the Senators present. Under the Constitution, as we all know, the President appoints certain officers of the United States, subject to confirmation by the Senate, conducts the foreign affairs of the Union, receives diplomatic agents from foreign countries, and negotiates treaties and conventions with them subject to the advice and consent of two-thirds of the Senators present.

In like manner there was no insurmountable difficulty in creating a Supreme Court of the Union, although there was considerable debate in reaching an agreement that the Congress might establish federal courts of first instance with an appeal to the Supreme Court. It was urged that all the States had courts, that it was therefore unnecessary to create new and competing ones, and that uniformity of interpretation of the Constitution, of Acts of Congress, of treaties of the United States, of constitutions and statutes of the several States, would be adequately secured on appeal to the Supreme Court about the advisability of whose creation there was neither doubt nor dispute. Assuredly, the State courts could have been utilized as suggested, but, as time has demonstrated, the system of federal courts created by the Congress and operating in every State and Territory has worked well, and the decisions of federal questions arising and corrected by the Supreme Court whenever the necessity arises.

INTERNATIONAL SIGNIFICANCE OF THE STATES OF THE UNION

These last matters, however, are familiar and of interest to the American, not necessarily to the foreigner. But Mr. Madison's Notes contain passages respecting the States, the Union of States, the relation of the laws of the Union to those of the several States, the judiciary, the nature of judicial questions, and the rôle that a court of Justice plays in this Union of States, and which it can therefore play in the Society of Nations. Such passages are of interest to American or foreigner believing not merely in the possibility, but in the absolute necessity, of international organization. The international aspect of these things has been strangely overlooked because of the tendency to regard the United States as a unitary nation, instead of a union of States, more perfect, indeed, than that of the Articles of Confederation, but nevertheless a union, for which the people of the several States ordained and estab-

Nation or Union of States.

lished this Constitution of the United States, to go no further than the Preamble to that venerable and venerated instrument of government. These phases of the subject will now be considered, for which Mr. Madison's Notes can be and must be taken as the first of texts and the most authentic of sources.

That we may rightly group the relations of the States to the Union let us consider again what was to be done. Twelve States had met by their delegates to create some form of Union more perfect than that existing under the Articles of Confederation, or to provide that Union with the powers to make its maintenance worth while. After the first day of the Convention the delegates were trying to endow a new Union of their own creation with a government, to carry out and to exercise the sovereign powers which the several States assembled in conference believed, as the Relation result of their experience, could be taken from of States each of them and transferred to the government Union. of the Union. This government was to be and still is the agent of the States for general purposes to the extent of the sovereign powers granted to it by the people of the several States. To this extent the Union is sovereign. The sovereign powers not granted, or which the States did not renounce, were to be and still are reserved to the several States. To remove any doubt on this subject, two articles to be added to the Constitution were proposed in the first session of the first Congress meeting under it, and, ratified by three-

fourths of the legislatures of 'the States then forming the Union, became an integral part of the
instrument. The first of the two Articles provides
that "The enumeration in the Constitution, of
certain rights, shall not be construed to deny or
disparage others retained by the people." The
second, that "The powers not delegated to the
United States by the Constitution, nor prohibited
by it to the States, are reserved to the States
respectively, or to the people."

We know that Mr. Madison approved of these
Articles because he proposed them to the Congress, and because in the course of the debates
he said so. The term "people," used in these two
articles added to the Constitution, and contained
in the opening words of the Preamble to the
Constitution, means the people of the States, not
"The the people generally without reference to the
People." States. While this is the reason of the thing, we
can nevertheless invoke the highest authority for
it, if authority be needed, for in delivering the
unanimous opinion of the Supreme Court of the
United States in the leading case, which is also
his masterpiece, of *McCulloch* v. *Maryland* (4
Wheaton, 316, 403), decided in 1819, the greatest
of Chief Justices, John Marshall, said:

No political dreamer was ever wild enough
to think of breaking down the lines which separate the States, and of compounding the American
people into one common mass.

The Chief Justice did not, however, leave the
matter here; he drew and stated the necessary con-

clusion of his thought and of his language, which was, be it remembered, likewise the view of his brethren, saying, " Of consequence, when they act, they act in their States."

We therefore have on the one hand the Union with its government of three branches, invested with sovereign powers of a general nature, conceived in the interest of the States as a whole, not in the interest of any one or group thereof, and to be exercised in the interest of all; and on the other hand, the governments of the several States, possessing and exercising the reserved sovereign powers of the States, or those whereof they did not renounce the exercise. Each, as Chief Justice Marshall has finely said in the McCulloch case, is sovereign within its proper sphere and neither sovereign within the proper sphere of the other.

Two sovereignties and their relation.

How were these two sovereignties to be kept in check, that is to say, each within its appropriate sphere? Mr. Madison and his closest friends first thought by investing the Union with the power to coerce the States to comply with their duties, to establish a council of revision to pass upon and to veto the acts of the States and of the Federal Legislature, contrary to the proposed Constitution. The discussion of these matters was long and interesting, and the details are given, no doubt faithfully, in his Notes by Mr. Madison, who records his repeated attempts to achieve his purpose in his own way, the repeated failures of himself and friends, and the method which fin- ally and fortunately prevailed, apparently the

The Supreme Law.

only method fitted for States of the Union and worthy of consideration by States of the Society of Nations. It is one of the most striking instances in which the conference was wiser than its wisest members. How was it done? By the simple expedient, as it seems to us of today, of making the Constitution, the laws of Congress made pursuant to it and the treaties of the United States, the supreme law of the Union, as of each of the States. In cases of controversy any or all of them may as written documents be passed upon, interpreted and applied, but only in a specific case arising thereunder duly carried to the court.

In the Virginian plan, undoubtedly drafted by Madison and still existing in his handwriting, the National Legislature was to be vested with the powers of the Congress under the Articles of Confederation and the right to legislate in cases in which the separate States were incompetent or involving the harmony of the Union.

In addition, and of especial importance for present purposes, the proposed National Legislature was to be possessed by the sixth resolution with the power and the right " to negative all laws passed by the several States, contravening in the opinion of the National Legislature the articles of Union; and to call forth the force of the Union agst any member of the Union failing to fulfill its duty under the articles thereof ".[1]

[1] *Documentary History of the Constitution,* vol. iii., p. 18.

THE SOCIETY OF NATIONS AND THE UNION
OF STATES

The eighth resolution of the Virginia plan
provided

that the Executive and a convenient number of
the National Judiciary, ought to compose a Council of Revision with authority to examine every A Court.
act of a National Legislature before it shall
operate, and every act of a particular Legislature
before a Negative thereon shall be final; and
that the dissent of the said Council shall amount
to a rejection, unless the Act of the National
Legislature be again passed, or that of a particular Legislature be again negatived by the members of each branch.[1]

There is no mention here of a court as such,
except that a number of judges were to act in an
advisory capacity upon measures which, if passed,
they might have to interpret and apply. But in
the course of the proceedings the court as such
made its appearance, replacing other provisions
which thereupon disappeared and are only to be
found in Mr. Madison's Notes, as they have
otherwise dropped entirely out of sight.

In the first place, the plan to coerce a State was Plan to
expressly discarded within two days of the intro- coerce
duction of the plan itself. On the 30th of May, rejected
Mr. Mason, according to Mr. Madison, "observed
that the present confederation was not only defi-

[1] *Documentary History of the Constitution*, vol. iii., pp. 18-19.

cient in not providing for coercion & punishment ag[st] delinquent States; but argued very cogently that punishment could not in the nature of things be executed on the States collectively, and therefore that such a Gov[t] was necessary as could directly operate on individuals, and would punish those only whose guilt required it."[1] This point of view evidently impressed Mr. Madison, because, the day after, he himself proposed to postpone this clause when it was reached in the first reading, saying, as reported by himself,

Coercion for individuals only. that the more he reflected on the use of force, the more he doubted the practicability, the justice and the efficacy of it when applied to people collectively, and not individually.— A Union of the States containing such an ingredient seemed to provide for its own destruction. The use of force ag[st] a State, would look more like a declaration of war, than an infliction of punishment, and would probably be considered by the party attacked as a dissolution of all previous compacts by which it might be bound. He hoped that such a system would be framed as might render this resource unnecessary, and moved that the clause be postponed.[2]

The motion was, as he says, "agreed to nem. con",[3] and the subject although subsequently brought before the conference in the session of June 15th, by the New Jersey plan, was not again seriously considered although it was discussed.

[1] *Documentary History of the Constitution*, vol. iii., p. 22.
[2] *Documentary History of the Constitution*, vol. iii., pp. 33-34.
[3] *Documentary History of the Constitution*, vol. iii., p. 34.

The clause ~~proposing~~ an action of the force of the whole of a delinquent State could not act on its constitution.

Mr. Madison, observed that the more he reflected on the use of force, the more he doubted the practicability, the justice and the efficacy of it when applied to people collectively and not individually. — An union of the States containing such an ingredient seemed to provide for its own destruction. The use of force against a State, would look more like a declaration of war, than an infliction of punishment, and would probably be considered by the party attacked as a dissolution of all previous compacts by which it might be bound. He hoped that such a system as would be found necessary to bind ——

The clause ~~~~ be further considered ——

This motion was agreed to nem. con.

The Committee then rose & the House adjourned

It is indeed true that the Articles of Confederation operated upon the individual in what may be considered minor matters, but in the essentials of government only upon the States themselves. The government of the perfected Union acts upon individuals in essentials and only incidentally, and in what may be considered exceptional cases, upon States. This was in form as well as in fact a reversal of the old order of things. This plan of Messrs. Mason and Madison fortunately prevailed, and the system of government ultimately adopted coerces the individual and controls the State by a declaration of the Supreme Court that the statute relied upon is not a defense to an individual acting upon and pleading it in justification of his action, as it is inconsistent with the Constitution, and, therefore, null and void. In the course of the session of July 14th, Mr. Madison "called for a single instance in which the Gen! Gov! was not to operate on the people individually."[1] Apparently none was given, as none is recorded in the notes, and Mr. Madison continued, expressing a truth so fundamental as to deserve to become an axiom of political science, that "the practicability of making laws, with coercive sanctions, for the States as political bodies, had been exploded on all hands."[2]

[1] *Documentary History of the Constitution,* vol. iii., p. 340.

In the 43d Number of *The Federalist,* which appeared on January 25, 1788, Mr. Madison recurred to this subject, and himself answered the question to which no reply had been given on the floor of the Convention.

[2] *Documentary History of the Constitution,* vol. iii., p. 340.

As already said, it was necessary to make of the Constitution, of the laws of Congress enacted in pursuance thereof, and of treaties, the supreme law alike of the Union and of the States. To accomplish this Mr. Madison left no stone unturned, and he completely succeeded, albeit after much difficulty. The expedient was exceedingly simple and effective, and is sufficiently stated for present purposes in the 15th and last resolution of the original Virginian plan, to the effect that the amendments which shall be offered to the Confederation by the Convention ought at a proper time, or times, after the approbation of Congress to be submitted to an assembly or assemblies of Representatives, recommended by the several Legislatures to be expressly chosen by the people, to consider & decide thereon. [1]

Basis of the Supreme Law.

The reasons for submitting the Constitution to the conventions of the people to be held in each of the States, specially called for this purpose, composed of members chosen by the people, not by the legislatures, were fully and frequently stated by Mr. Madison during the course of the debates on this question, which he regarded, and rightly, as of fundamental importance. Of the many statements of Madison and his followers, three made in three different periods of the Convention will suffice. Early in its sessions,

Mr. Madison [as recorded by himself, under date of June 5th] thought this provision essential. The articles of Confed.ᵖ themselves were defec-

[1] *Documentary History of the Constitution*, vol. iii., p. 20.

tive in this respect, resting in many of the States on the Legislative sanction only. Hence in conflicts between acts of the States, and of Cong? especially where the former are of posterior date, and the decision is to be made by State Tribunals, an uncertainty must necessarily prevail, or rather perhaps a certain decision in favor of State authority. He suggested also that as far as the articles of Union were to be considered as a Treaty only of a particular sort, among the Governments of Independent States, the doctrine might be set up that a breach of any one article, by any of the parties, absolved the other parties from the whole obligation. For these reasons as well as others he thought it indispensable that the new Constitution should be ratified in the most unexceptional form, and by the supreme authority of the people themselves.[1]

Later when the matter was up again in the session of July 23rd,

Mr. Madison thought it clear that the Legislatures were incompetent to the proposed changes. These changes would make essential inroads on the State Constitutions, and it would be a novel & dangerous doctrine that a Legislature could change the constitution under which it held its existence. There might indeed be some constitutions within the Union, which had given a power to the Legislature to concur in alterations of the federal Compact. But there were certainly some which had not; and in the case of these, a ratification must of necessity be obtained from the people. He considered the difference between a system founded on the Legis-

[1] *Documentary History of the Constitution,* vol. iii., pp. 65-66.

latures only, and one founded on the people, to be the true difference between a *league* or *treaty,* and a *Constitution.* The former in point of *moral obligation* might be as inviolable as the latter. In point of *political operation,* there were two important distinctions in favor of the latter. 1. A law violating a treaty ratified by a pre-existing law, might be respected by the Judges as a law, though an unwise & perfidious one. A law violating a constitution established by the people themselves, would be considered by the Judges as null & void. 2. The doctrine laid down by the law of Nations in the case of treaties is that a breach of any one article by any of the parties, frees the other parties from their engagements. In the case of a union of people under one Constitution, the nature of the pact has always been understood to exclude such an interpretation. Comparing the two modes in point of expediency he thought all the considerations which recommended this Convention in preference to Congress for proposing the reform were in favor of State Conventions in preference to the Legislatures for examining and adopting it.[1]

Finally, in the session of August 31st,

Mr. Madison considered it best to require Conventions; Among other reasons, for this, that the powers given to the Gen! Gov! were being taken from the State Gov!ˢ the Legislatures would be more disinclined than conventions composed in part at least of other men; and if disinclined, they could devise modes apparently promoting, but really thwarting the ratification. The diffi-

[1] *Documentary History of the Constitution,* vol. iii., p. 411.

culty in Maryland was no greater than in other States, where no mode of change was pointed out by the Constitution, and all officers were under oath to support it. The people were in fact, the fountain of all power, and by resorting to them, all difficulties were got over. They could alter constitutions as they pleased. It was a principle in the Bills of rights, that first principles might be resorted to.[1]

The meaning of all this is eminently clear and free from reasonable doubt. By the Declaration of Independence, the people were henceforward to be regarded as the source of power. The proposed Constitution for all the States was drafted by the delegates of all the States. The constitution of each State dealing with questions arising within and not extending beyond the confines of the State, was drafted by delegates of the State. The Constitution of the United States was to be ratified by the people of each of the States in order to bind each of the States. The State constitution was to be ratified only by the people of that State. Each State was thus to have two constitutions each ratified by the source of power, namely the people. Each State with two Constitutions.

If matters had stood here, each constitution, National and State, would have been of equal rank and validity. But all doubts are removed by other considerations. The New Jersey plan, proposed on June 15th by Mr. Paterson of that State, in behalf of the smaller States, although

[1] *Documentary History of the Constitution*, vol. iii., p. 656.

rejected, contained an article which, amended in form but adopted in substance, provided

that all Acts of the U. States in Cong: made by virtue & in pursuance of the powers hereby & by the articles of confederation vested in them, and all Treaties made & ratified under the authority of the U. States shall be the supreme law of the respective States so far forth as those Acts or Treaties shall relate to the said States or their Citizens, and that the Judiciary of the several States shall be bound thereby in their decisions, any thing in the respective laws of the Individual States to the contrary notwithstanding.[1]

If we combine this clause, which as amended forms the second edition of Article VI, of the Constitution, with the first clause of the second section of Article III, extending the judicial power of the United States " to all Cases, in Law and Equity, arising under this Constitution, the Laws of the United States, and Treaties made, or which shall be made, under their Authority," we have the full demonstration of the problem. The Constitution, Acts of Congress, and treaties are not only the law, but the supreme law, of the Union and of each of the several States, and to be held as such by all courts, State and Federal.

To the student of international conferences interested to know how our forefathers of that day settled the questions of revision, constitutionality, amendments and withdrawal from the

Supreme Law of both States and Union.

---

[1] *Documentary History of the Constitution,* vol. iii., pp. 127-128.

Union, only a few words are necessary. In the Revision. Constitution there is no place for a council of revision, but the President was given the power to veto an act of Congress unless passed again by a two-thirds majority in each house. Its con- Constitutionality is to be determined by the judges tionality. not acting in an advisory capacity but as judges in the decision of a given case arising under the law. "A junction of the judiciary" would, as John Dickinson aptly said in the session of June 6th, involve "an improper mixture of powers."[1] It was natural that the State judges should pass upon the question of repugnance to the supreme law, especially because the Federal Constitution was likewise the constitution of the State, and the supreme law. Since the Constitu- Amendtion was adopted in its entirety by the people of ments. each of the several States, it was not only the supreme law, but it could only be amended, and the relations between the Union and the States changed, by the legislatures or conventions of three-fourths of the States, in accordance with the Fifth Article. There is here, therefore, no room for withdrawal, for the people of a State could only change its relations to the Union by the vote of three-fourths of the States. It Secesis difficult to see how the people of a State could sion. withdraw from their own Constitution, which they themselves and in conjunction with the other States had made their supreme law. Secession could only be revolution.

[1] *Documentary History of the Constitution,* vol. iii., p. 79.

While it is technically correct to say that the
Constitution was made by delegates of twelve
States, it was nevertheless true that its framers
contemplated that Rhode Island, which was not
represented, would consent to ratify it and thus
make the more perfect union coterminous with
the English colonies of the New World which
had proclaimed their independence on July 4,
1776, and whose recognition as States was acknowledged by the mother country on September
3, 1783. It was foreseen, however, that the territory to the westward, which had been ceded to
the United States by the States claiming it, would
be peopled by the venturesome of the East or
their descendants; that this territory would be
subdivided, and, at the instance and request of
the inhabitants, admitted as States to the Union
of States upon what terms? As equals or in-
feriors? The far-sighted, of whom Mr. Mason,
Mr. Madison and Mr. Sherman were conspicuous
examples, urged their admission upon equality.
Gouverneur Morris, however, and some others,
wishing to maintain the supremacy of the Atlantic seaboard at the expense of the inland and
Western States, opposed this, with the result that
the third section of the Fourth Article of the
Constitution merely provides that " New States
may be admitted by the Congress into this Union,"
without, however, stating that the admission was
to be upon terms of equality with the other members. But the spirit if not the letter required it,
and in practice every State is admitted upon a

Admission of new States. *(margin note)*

basis of equality, so that the latest newcomer stands upon the same footing with the States that gained their independence from Great Britain and which made the Constitution of the United States in the Federal Convention of 1787 a possibility. No other solution of the problem is conceivable in this more perfect union of the western world; no other solution should be possible in a perfected Society of Nations.

RELATION OF JUSTICIABLE TO POLITICAL QUESTIONS

The judicial power of the United States extends only to justiciable, not political questions, as was pointed out by Mr. Madison in the session of August 27th. He "doubted whether it was not going too far to extend the jurisdiction of the Court generally to cases arising Under the Constitution & whether it ought not to be limited to cases of a Judiciary Nature. The right of expounding the Constitution in cases not of this nature ought not to be given to that Department."[1] And Mr. Madison was doubtless correct when he says it was "generally supposed that the jurisdiction given was constructively limited to cases of a Judiciary nature."[2] Such was the view of the conference, such is the view repeatedly expressed by the Supreme Court itself. How the unconstitutionality of an act and the

[1] *Documentary History of the Constitution*, vol. iii., p. 626.
[2] *Documentary History of the Constitution*, vol. iii., p. 626.

justiciable nature of a controversy are to be determined are matters of such international importance as well as of domestic concern that they may well be examined with some care.

In regard to the first matter, it may be said at once that the function of the court in cases The unconstitutionality of an act. involving the constitutionality of an act as understood in the American Union is not recognized elsewhere, although our method seems essential to the success if not to the conception of a Federation.   The English view, prevailing it is believed generally, except in the more perfect Union of the United States, and in such Federations as the Dominion of Canada and the Commonwealth of Australia, is shortly stated by Mr. Justice Willes, who, in speaking of an act of Parliament and the course which an English court of justice may take in reference to it, said, in the case of *Lee* v. *Bude and Torrington Junction Railway* (Law Reports, 6 Common Pleas Division, 576), decided in 1871:

I would observe, as to these Acts of Parliament, that they are the law of this land; and we do not sit here as a court of appeal from parliament.   It was once said—I think in Hobart[1]— that, if an Act of Parliament were to create a man judge in his own case, the Court might disregard it.   That dictum, however, stands as a

[1] The case to which Mr. Justice Willes refers is, as stated in a note to the opinion, that of *Day* v. *Savadge* (Hob. Art. 87), in which that learned Judge is reported by himself to have said: "Even an Act of Parliament made against natural equity, as, to make a man judge in his own case, is void in itself; for, *jura naturae sunt immutabilia,* and they are *leges legum.*"

warning, rather than an authority to be followed. We sit here as servants of the Queen and the legislature. Are we to act as regents over what is done by Parliament with the consent of the Queen, lords, and commons? I deny that any such authority exists. If an Act of Parliament has been obtained improperly, it is for the legislature to correct it by repealing it: but, so long as it exists as law, the Courts are bound to obey it. The proceedings here are judicial, not autocratic, which they would be if we could make laws instead of administering them.

But there was nevertheless English precedent for the American way, with which the colonists were familiar, and indeed there were some three American precedents within the personal or professional knowledge of the lawyer members of the Convention.

It was a principle of the English common law that an act of a corporation in excess of the grant in its articles of incorporation was *ultra vires,* and as such null and void; and it was also a principle of the common law, that by-laws of a corporation could not be valid and yet contrary to the laws of England, without a statement by the law-making power to that effect. It was further a principle of the common law that the king himself could not authorize a corporation to pass a by-law contrary to the law of the realm. The importance of these principles will appear if it be noted that the colonies were bodies politic and political corporations, and therefore any act of a colonial assembly repugnant to the laws of

England was null, void and of no effect. It could be disallowed by the king in council, and a decision of the colonial court based upon the law could be reversed by the king in council. The leading case on the subject was that of *Withrop* v. *Lechmere* (7 Connecticut Colonial Records, 571), decided in 1728, in which the king in council held, upon appeal from a Connecticut court, that a statute of that colony modifying the course of inheritance contrary to the common law of England was null and void, and the decisions of Connecticut courts based upon it were accordingly reversed. The case was clear, as the charter of Connecticut only authorized that body politic "to Make, Ordain, and Establish all Manner of Wholesome and Reasonable Laws, Statutes, Ordinances, Directions, and Instructions, not Contrary to the Laws of this Realm, of England." The Constitution of the Union and of each of the several States was in these respects like the charter of the colony.

There were, however, three American cases laying down the same doctrine: *Holmes* v. *Walton* (4 American Historical Review, 456), decided in 1780 by the Supreme Court of New Jersey; *Trevett* v. *Weeden* (Coxe, Judicial Power and Unconstitutional Legislation, 234), decided in 1786 by the Supreme Court of Rhode Island, and *Bayard* v. *Singleton* (1 Martin, N. C. 48). In the first two of these cases a law of the legislators was declared unconstitutional as contrary to the constitution of the one, and the charter of the other, for Rhode Island continued to live until 1842 under the Royal Charter of 1663; and in the third, the court of North Carolina not only held a State statute contrary to the Constitution to be null and void, but also declared the Articles of Confederation to be the supreme law of that State.

The great and leading case on the subject upholding this view is that of *Marbury* v. *Madison* (1 Cranch, 137, 177-178, 180), decided in 1803, in which Chief Justice Marshall, speaking for the Supreme Court of the Union, declared an Act of Congress unconstitutional as inconsistent with the Constitution, saying:

Certainly all those who have framed written constitutions contemplate them as forming the fundamental and paramount law of the nation, and consequently the theory of every such government must be, that an act of the legislature, repugnant to the constitution, is void. This theory is essentially attached to a written constitution and is consequently to be considered, by this court, as one of the fundamental principles of our society. It is not, therefore, to be lost sight of in the further consideration of this subject.

If an act of the legislature, repugnant to the constitution, is void, does it, notwithstanding its invalidity, bind the courts, and oblige them to give it effect? Or, in other words, though it be not law, does it constitute a rule as operative as if it was a law? This would be to overthrow in fact, what was established in theory; and would seem, at first view, an absurdity too gross to be insisted on. It shall, however, receive a more attentive consideration.

It is emphatically the province and duty of the judicial department, to say what the law is. Those who apply the rule to particular cases, must of necessity expound and interpret that rule. If two laws conflict with each other, the courts must decide on the operation of each.

So if a law be in opposition to the constitution; if both the law and the constitution apply to a particular case, so that the court must either decide that case conformably to the law, disregarding the constitution; or conformably to the constitution, disregarding the law; the court must determine which of these conflicting rules governs the case. This is of the very essence of judicial duty.

If then the courts are to regard the constitution; and the constitution is superior to any ordinary act of the legislature, the constitution, and not such ordinary act, must govern the case to which they both apply . . .

It is also not entirely unworthy of observation, that in declaring what shall be the *supreme* law of the land, the constitution itself is first mentioned; and not the laws of the United States, generally, but those only which shall be made in *pursuance* of the constitution, have that rank.

If the judicial power only extends to judicial and not to political cases, it becomes of importance **Difference** to define the distinction between them. This the **between** Supreme Court has done in a long line of cases, **Judicial** among which may be mentioned the following: **and** *Foster* v. *Neilson* (2 Peters, 253), decided in **Political** **cases.**

1829; *Williams* v. *Suffolk Insurance Company* (13 Peters, 415), decided in 1839; *Luther* v. *Borden* (7 Howard, 1), decided in 1849; *the Prize Cases* (2 Black, 635), decided in 1862; *State of Mississippi* v. *Johnson* (4 Wallace, 475), decided in 1866; *State of Georgia* v. *Stanton* (6 Wallace, 50), decided in 1867, and *Pacific Telephone Company* v. *State of Oregon* (223 U. S. 118), decided in 1912. With these cases at his disposal the foreign as well as the American publicist can readily appreciate the distinction, and it is therefore a confession of ignorance to maintain that the distinction can not be laid down by a court with precision. It is a manifestation of repugnance to judicial decision to contend that the foreign government must determine this question for itself on the ground that a court of justice is incompetent in the premises.

But if a political question must always remain political, and can not become justiciable so as to fall within the domain of the judicial power, and thus within the jurisdiction of a court of justice, the usefulness of an international court is indeed limited, although within its sphere it may justify its creation a thousand times over by the decision of justiciable disputes between nations. A political question may, however, become justiciable. It is within the power of any two nations to make it so between themselves. It is therefore within the power of the nations of the Society of Nations to make it so between and among themselves. The Supreme Court of

How political questions may become judicial.

the United States has so held, and has stated the
method with the precision of the judge and the
vision of the statesman, in the case of *The State
of Rhode Island* v. *The State of Massachusetts*
(12 Peters, 657, 736-8), decided in 1838, in
which Mr. Justice Baldwin, delivering the opinion of his brethren, said:

**Mr.
Justice
Baldwin.**

The founders of our government could not
but know, what has ever been, and is familiar
to every statesman and jurist, that all controversies between nations, are, in this sense, political,
and not judicial, as none but the sovereign can
settle them. In the declaration of independence,
the states assumed their equal station among the
powers of the earth, and asserted that they could
of right do, what other independent states could
do; "declare war, make peace, contract alliances;" of consequence, to settle their controversies with a foreign power, or among themselves, which no state, and no power could do for
them. They did contract an alliance with France,
in 1778; and with each other, in 1781: the
object of both was to defend and secure their
asserted rights as states; but they surrendered
to congress, and its appointed Court, the right
and power of settling their mutual controversies;
thus making them judicial questions, whether they
arose on "boundary, jurisdiction, or any other
cause whatever." There is neither the authority
of law or reason for the position, that boundary
between nations or states, is, in its nature, any
more a political question, than any other subject on which they may contend. None can be
settled without war or treaty, which is by political power; but under the old and new confed-

eracy they could and can be settled by a court constituted by themselves, as their own substitutes, authorized to do that for states, which states alone could do before. We are thus pointed to the true boundary line between political and judicial power, and questions. A sovereign decides by his own will, which is the supreme law within his own boundary; 6 Peters 714; 9 Peters 748; a court, or judge, decides according to the law prescribed by the sovereign power, and that law is the rule for judgment. The submission by the sovereigns, or states, to a court of law or equity, of a controversy between them, without prescribing any rule of decision, gives power to decide according to the appropriate law of the case; 11 Ves. 294; which depends on the subject matter, the source and nature of the claims of the parties, and the law which governs them. From the time of such submission, the question ceases to be a political one, to be decided by the sic volo, sic jubeo, of political power; it comes to the court to be decided by its judgment, legal discretion, and solemn consideration of the rules of law appropriate to its nature as a judicial question, depending on the exercise of judicial power; as it is bound to act by known and settled principles of national or municipal jurisprudence, as the case requires. . . .

These considerations lead to the definition of political and judicial power and questions; the former is that which a sovereign or state exerts by his or its own authority, as reprisal and confiscation; 3 Ves. 429: the latter is that which is granted to a court or judicial tribunal. So of controversies between states; they are in their nature political, when the sovereign or state reserves to itself the right of deciding on it;

makes it the "subject of a treaty, to be settled as between states independent," or " the foundation of representations from state to state." This is political equity, to be adjudged by the parties themselves, as contradistinguished from judicial equity, administered by a court of justice, decreeing the equum et bonum of the case, let who or what be the parties before them.

From this remarkable utterance it is clear that should the Society of Nations or any considerable number of the nations be minded to take the step, it would not be a leap in the dark, nor would it be even an experiment. The Philadelphia Convention showed how easily the step may be taken, and the Supreme Court has by the practice and procedure of a century in the matter of controversies between States furnished the precedents which men of good will may heed. All of the nations do not need to agree to form an international tribunal, for the American plan of a more perfect Union was to go into effect when nine of the States should ratify the Constitution, and it is fundamental to bear in mind that by the express language of the Constitution, only those States were to be bound which did so ratify it. Nor is it necessary, on the other hand, that the nations form themselves into a Union of States for all, or even for general purposes, as States united for judicial settlement will suffice for justiciable purposes. They merely need to agree by treaty, convention, compact, call it what you will, to submit their disputes,

A lesson for the Society of Nations.

heretofore unsettled by their diplomatic agents, to a court of their own creation, and therefore their agent for this purpose. In the impressive language of Mr. Justice Baldwin the dispute would be " settled by a court constituted by themselves, as their substitutes authorized to do that for the States, which States alone could do before," according to the appropriate law of the case, depending upon " the subject matter, the source and nature of the claims of the parties, and the law which governs them," and according to " its judgment, legal discretion, and solemn consideration of the rules of law appropriate to its nature as a judicial question, depending on the exercise of judicial power; as it is bound to act by known and settled principles of national or municipal jurisprudence as the case requires."

The illustration by which the learned justice enforces his views is not only apt, but unanswerable, showing the vast extent and nature of the domain already subjected to judicial settlement. Thus he says:

It has never been contended that prize courts of admiralty jurisdiction, or questions before them, are not strictly judicial; they decide on questions of war and peace, the law of nations, treaties, and the municipal laws of the capturing nation, by which alone they are constituted; a fortiori, if such courts were constituted by a solemn treaty between the State under whose authority the capture was made, and the State whose citizens or subjects suffer by the capture. All nations submit to the jurisdiction of such courts over their subjects, and hold their final decrees conclusive on rights of property. 6 Cr. 284-5.

What had been done in the matter of prize, the framers of the Constitution did in other disputes between States of a kind and nature to be decided in a court of justice in accordance with Mr. Justice Baldwin's views by the simple, practicable and highly successful expedient of extending the judicial power of the United States—or if you please, of the Society of Nations, or of the contracting parties—" to controversies between two or more States," which because of this extension become " of a Judiciary nature," to use Mr. Madison's expression, already quoted in another connection.

Lest the process may seem too simple, or too easy, it is wise to yield the floor again to Mr. Justice Baldwin, who says in an earlier portion of the opinion of the Supreme Court in the Rhode Island and Massachusetts case (12 Peters, 654, 720):

Those states, in their highest sovereign capacity, in the convention of the people thereof; on whom, by the revolution, the prerogative of the crown, and the transcendent power of parliament devolved, in a plenitude unimpaired by any act, and controllable by no authority, 6 Wheat. 651; 8 Wheat. 584, 88; adopted the constitution, by which they respectively made to the United States a grant of judiciary power over controversies between two or more states. By the con-

Jurisdiction by consent and delegated authority.

stitution, it was ordained that this judicial power, in cases where a state was a party, should be exercised by this Court as one of original jurisdiction. The states waived their exemption from judicial power, 6 Wheat. 378, 80, as sovereigns by original and inherent right, by their own grant of its exercise over themselves in such cases, but which they would not grant to any inferior tribunal. By this grant, this Court has acquired jurisdiction over the parties in this cause, by their own consent and delegated authority; as their agent for executing the judicial power of the United States in the cases specified.

Will the sovereign States of the Society of Nations obstinately refuse to follow the path beaten out and marked by the sovereign States of the New World, which recognized that between diplomacy and war, which they renounced, there is only war? The question is not what existed before the meeting of the States in conference in Philadelphia, in the year of grace 1787. It is no longer necessary to *originate,* it is only necessary to *follow,* for the wise men of that day and generation and of that Convention made State suable by State, and in the course of a hundred years of litigation both the practice and procedure to be followed are spread before the nations, not figuratively as in an open book, but literally in a series of books known as the Reports of the Supreme Court of the United States, which their rulers can purchase for a few paltry dollars and master in their moments of leisure to their enduring benefit between the

A light unto the world.

maneuvers of their armies and the reviews of their fleets.

The desire expressed by Richard Caswell, Governor of the State of North Carolina, in a letter dated July 26, 1787, addressed to Mr. R. D. Spaight, a delegate of that State in attendance upon the Convention, for " an independent Judicial department to decide any contest that may happen between the United States and individual States & between one State and another," [1] has been more than realized. State has appeared against State in the Supreme Court of the States, and the judges of that court have decided, after argument of counsel and mature reflection on their part, many a controversy which would have been a cause for war if it had been between disunited States, instead of between members of united States.

As was to be expected, from the looseness with which their charters were drawn, the boundaries of the States gave rise to litigation in the Supreme Court, just as they had given rise to dispute between the colonies, and were settled by the king in council. There were eleven such disputes outstanding between and among the States when the government under the Constitution went into effect. For a number of years thereafter, the only controversies between the States in which the jurisdiction of the Supreme Court was invoked related to boundary, and the first final decision

[1] North Carolina State Records, xx, 753; quoted from Farrand, *Records of the Federal Convention of 1787*, vol. iii., p. 64.

in a case of this kind was rendered as late as
1846, between Rhode Island and Massachusetts,
which latter State, curiously enough, objected to
the jurisdiction of the court, which, however and
notwithstanding, decided in its favor.[1] As the
result of confidence in judicial decision, some
thirty-one of the forty-eight States now composing
the Union have been plaintiff or defendant at
one time or another in controversies between and
among them. The United States, itself, has
appeared at the bar of the Supreme Court, and
has filed its complaint against more than one of
these united States. From boundary disputes,
the jurisdiction of the court has been invoked
in cases of contract, in differences concerning
riparian right, in matters affecting the health
and well-being of their inhabitants; and in the
course of time State will doubtless appear against
State in every kind of a dispute arising between
them, which can be presented to a court, because
there is no limit to litigation between States recognizing the principles of justice and willing to
conform to the rule of law.

The eighty-odd decisions of the Supreme Court
of the " several States," to use the language of
the conference, in controversies between them,
remove the question of the feasibility of such a
tribunal from the field of academic discussion,
making of it simply a concrete matter of worldly
and of political wisdom.

There is little in Madison's Notes on this " in-

[1] *State of Rhode Island* v. *State of Massachusetts,* 4 Howard, 591.

teresting matter" as it would have been called by the framers of the Constitution. Every State

had the threefold division of sovereign powers. Every State had its judiciary. That the Union was to have one apparently went without saying—at least there is no evidence that this phase of the subject was debated or that it even gave rise to any difference of opinion. Indeed, there is next to nothing on the matter of controversies between States. Diplomacy had failed to settle their many and difficult disputes, and war they would not have, for they were unwilling like Saturn to be devoured by their own offspring. In colonial times disputes between the colonies all independent of one another and all without tribunals of their own to which they might defer as of right their "Judiciary" cases, were, however, in default of a supreme court of the colonies carried to the Privy Council in England, where they were settled by that due process of law which hears before it determines, and decides according to the law of the case. Indeed, three of the boundaries of Rhode Island—the fourth is the ocean—have been fixed, two by judicial decree of the Privy Council of colonial days, at the instance of Rhode Island against Connecticut and Massachusetts,[1] and one later under the more perfect Union, by a decision of the Supreme Court in a controversy between Rhode Island and

[1] *Colony of Rhode Island* v. *Colony of Connecticut* (3 Acts of the Privy Council, Colonial Series, 10), decided in 1727; *Colony of Rhode Island* v. *Colony of Massachusetts* (3 Acts of the Privy Council, Colonial Series, 436), decided in 1746.

Massachusetts.[1] The erstwhile colonists invested the Congress under the Articles of Confederation with this portion of the jurisdiction formerly exercised by the Privy Council, and devised a method of appointing commissioners for the temporary courts, who were to decide " all disputes and differences " then existing or afterward arising " between two or more States concerning boundary, jurisdiction or any other cause whatever." The principles of judicial procedure were readily acceptable to the framers of the Constitution because beyond the pale of controversy.

In the Virginian plan the national judiciary was to have jurisdiction of " questions which may involve the national peace and harmony." In section 3 of the Eleventh Article of the first draft of the Constitution reported by the Committee of Detail on August 6th, the judicial power of the United States was extended to " controversies between two or more States," excepting therefrom such as regarded " Territory or Jurisdiction." [2] These, as involving the sovereignty of the States were, by the Ninth Article of the draft, to be referred to the Senate, representing the States as such, just as they were and for a like reason referred to the Congress under the Ninth of the Articles of Confederation. This cause was taken up in the session of August 24th

---

[1] *State of Rhode Island* v. *State of Massachusetts* (4 Howard, 591), decided in 1846.
[2] *Documentary History of the Constitution,* vol. iii., p. 454.

and was quickly disposed of, Mr. Rutledge of
South Carolina, soon to be appointed Chief Justice of the Supreme Court, saying, according to
Mr. Madison, that " this provision for deciding
controversies between the States was necessary
under the Confederation, but will be rendered
unnecessary by the National Judiciary now to
be established, and moved to strike it out."[1]   Dr.
Johnson, a wise and able delegate and experienced
lawyer from Connecticut, who had tried and lost
the case of Connecticut against Pennsylvania,[2] the
one case tried by a temporary commission under
the Articles of Confederation, seconded the
motion, in which Mr. Sherman, likewise a
lawyer from Connecticut, " concurred."[3]   Mr.
Williamson, a physician of North Carolina, had
his doubts it would seem, and favored " postponing instead of striking out, in order to consider
whether this might not be a good provision, in
cases where the Judiciary were interested or too
closely connected with the parties "[4]; Mr. Gorham, a merchant of Massachusetts, also " had
doubts as to striking out, the Judges might be
connected with the States being parties.   He was
inclined to think the mode proposed in the clause
would be more satisfactory than to refer such
cases to the Judiciary."[5]   Only New Hampshire,
North Carolina and Georgia voted for postpone-

[1] *Documentary History of the Constitution,* vol. iii., p. 607.
[2] 131 U. S., Appendix, p. liv., decided in 1781.
[3] *Documentary History of the Constitution,* vol. iii., p. 607.
[4] *Documentary History of the Constitution,* vol. iii., p. 607.
[5] *Documentary History of the Constitution,* vol. iii., p. 607.

ment; whereupon Mr. Wilson, a distinguished lawyer of Pennsylvania, who had won the case for his State in its controversy with Connecticut in which Dr. Johnson had appeared for that State against him, " urged the striking out, the Judiciary being a better provision."[1] Only North Carolina and Georgia stood by Mr. Gorham, whose State voted against him, and the Supreme Court of the Union was vested with jurisdiction in controversies between the several States thereof, with only a constructive exception of those of " a judiciary nature " again to use Mr. Madison's phrase.

There was, however, a further category of controversies contained in the Articles of Confederation, but not submitted to the Court in the first draft of the Constitution. This was discovered by the keen and penetrating eye of Mr. Sherman, who proposed in the session of August 27th, with the unanimous approval of the Convention, to invest the court with " jurisdiction of causes ' between Citizens of the same State claiming lands under grants of different States,' according to the provision in the 9th art. of the Confederation."[2]

The Supreme Court therefore became the legitimate successor of the Privy Council and Congress, and because of this we are privileged to repeat, it offers the nations a model and a hope of judicial settlement of their controversies

Again the international significance.

---

[1] *Documentary History of the Constitution,* vol. iii., p. 608.
[2] *Documentary History of the Constitution,* vol. iii., p. 627.

which, if they are to be got out of the way after the breakdown of diplomacy, can only be settled by war. If the nations only will, they may make a union of any of their number for judicial settlement, and that by simply a treaty, convention, compact or agreement, creating the court, granting it jurisdiction, defining its procedure, to be set in motion by the plaintiff, leaving the execution of the judgment as in the case of an arbitral award or of a decision of our Supreme Court to the good faith of the contracting parties, and it is done. The example of the American States shows the way to do it. The procedure of the court of the several States shows the feasibility of doing it. The agony of Europe shows that it must be done if the blood and treasure of the future are to be saved from the catastrophes of the past.

And what is, after all, this more perfect Union of the American States, whose formation Mr.
The more perfect union or Society of Nations. Madison records in his Notes, that it should be held up as an example or as a model to the Society of Nations? Let the Articles of Union answer that it was ordained, as specifically set forth in the Preamble, " to establish Justice, insure domestic Tranquillity, provide for the common defence, promote the general Welfare, and secure the Blessings of Liberty to ourselves and our Posterity." What the States of the New World have done, the nations of the Old World can afford to consider, even although they be unwilling or find it impos-

sible to endow their union, society, association, or league with such extensive powers or prerogatives.

The problem which faced the States faces the nations. How can each of them divest itself of certain sovereign powers to be used for the common good of all, not in the interest of any one, without merging the nations in a union in which they shall become as provinces? Were not the Americans of the several States one people, it may be asked? Was not the union made by the people as such, irrespective of States, forming a nation with all the sovereign powers of such, and in which the States are as counties, or shires, departments or provinces of a unitary nation? To this it may be briefly said that the union is one of States; that the word " nation " is not to be found in the Constitution; that the people of the States, acting as citizens of the States and within State lines, not the people generally compounded as one mass, created the more perfect union, as the Constitution says, and that the States which compose this union are States of a composite nation, if the term " nation " must be used in preference to the language of the Constitution.

But however this may be, the nations do not need to go so far as the States of the American Union. They may prefer that the society of which they are the component parts shall remain a very loose union. But the framework is at hand, for is not the Society of Nations already

Certain parallels. a union which needs only to become conscious of its existence to be made more perfect? And however many or few the powers granted by the nations, it will assuredly, indeed inevitably, be more limited than the more perfect union of the American States, even though that was and still is a limited union. Is not the Hague Peace Conference something very much like a legislature *ad referendum*—a body that drafts and proposes projects for the nations to accept or reject? Is not the so-called Permanent Court of Arbitration something like the temporary commissions under the Articles of Confederation and a first step to a judiciary of the Society of Nations " accessible to all, in the midst of the independent Powers "?

If some committee were thought desirable between the regular and stated meetings of the conference, the so-called Permanent Administrative Council would suffice, with such added functions as experience should suggest, " composed," as it is, " of the diplomatic representatives of the signatory Powers accredited to The Hague and of the Netherland Minister for Foreign Affairs " as President," to be charged with the direction and control of such business of the Union of Society as the contracting Powers might consider it safe to entrust to a council of this nature. But if the Society of Nations be consciously reorganized or strengthened, such limited powers as it may possess should operate upon the individual as in the more perfect Union of the American States, by giving the provisions of the Convention the force of law, to be ratified if need be by the people of the States, thus taxing a person, not a nation, with the performance of a duty, or abstinence from an act, instead of a State, as otherwise the problem of coercing a country—that is to say, war—might arise.

No State if possible, certainly no powerful one, should be invested with the right or duty of supervising or executing the terms of the agreement of the nations. The success of the American experiment is, it is believed, due in no small measure to the fact that no State of the Union is President thereof, and also to the fact that no limited power of the union is placed under the guarantee or protection of any one State, such as Massachusetts, Pennsylvania, or Virginia, but in a government of the Union, without territory of its own other than a few square miles constituting the District of Columbia, in which the government of the Union lives, moves and has its being. Inevitably or ordinarily the *primus inter pares* ends by swallowing up its equals of the beginning.

Neither national nor federal.

Of the nature of the Union, let Mr. Madison speak, who had more to do with its making than any one man, but whose opinion in any event is of itself entitled to great and deserved weight. In the thirty-eighth number of *The Federalist,* a series of papers written by Mr. Hamilton, Mr. Madison and Mr. Jay, shortly after the adjournment of the Convention and in order to influence the States to ratify the Constitution, Mr. Madison said:

The proposed Constitution, therefore, is, in strictness, neither a national nor a federal Constitution, but a composition of .both. In its foundation it is federal, not national; in the sources from which the ordinary powers of the government are drawn, it is partly federal and partly national; in the operation of these powers, it is national, not federal: in the extent of them, again, it is federal, not national; and, finally, in the authoritative mode of introducing amendments, it is neither wholly federal nor wholly national.

We Americans would like to think and to express the thought, although it may seem immodest, perhaps even boastful, that the Constitution of the more perfect Union has the virtue and strength of each, with the vice and weakness of neither.

Foreign students of our Constitution are apt to be confused by the phraseology of the Preamble to that instrument. The opening sentence **The Preamble and its limitations.** of, or Preamble to the Constitution is a flourish of rhetoric due to a facile pen, not a grant of power made by the States, which is only conveyed in the body of the Constitution. When the first draft thereof was reported in the session of August 6th, the opening sentence and the First Article, later wisely and happily compressed into the Preamble, were thus worded:

We the people of the States of New Hampshire, Massachusetts, Rhode-Island and Providence

Plantations, Connecticut, New-York, New-Jersey, Pennsylvania, Delaware, Maryland, Virginia, North-Carolina, South-Carolina, and Georgia, do ordain, declare, and establish the following Constitution for the Government of Ourselves and our Posterity.

The stile of the Government shall be " The United States of America ". [1]

Under date of August 7th, Mr. Madison informs us that " the preamble of the Report was agreed to nem. con. So were Art. I & II," [2] the latter to the effect that the government was to consist of a legislative, executive and judicial department. Without further discussion and with no changes in the Preamble and First Article, the Constitution as amended after weeks of debate was submitted to a Committee on Style and Arrangement, elected by ballot in the session of September 8th, consisting " of M⸢ Johnson, M⸢ Hamilton, M⸢ Gov⸢ Morris, M⸢ Madison and M⸢ King ". [3]

This was an excellent committee and the presence upon it of Mr. Madison—the only committee of which he was a member—made it a certainty that no change of style would affect the sense of the document, with which he was more familiar than any other member could be, if only from his self-imposed duty as reporter.

The Convention adjourned Saturday, September 8th, shortly after the appointment of the

[1] *Documentary History of the Constitution*, vol. iii., p. 444.
[2] *Documentary History of the Constitution*, vol. iii., p. 458.
[3] *Documentary History of the Constitution*, vol. iii., p. 710.

committee, and met on Monday, the 10th, which Messrs. Hamilton, King and Madison attended and in whose proceedings they participated. Messrs. Johnson and Gouverneur Morris were either absent or failed to take part in the proceedings; they were probably busied with the "stile" and arrangement of the Constitution.

On Tuesday, the 11th, the committee reported the Constitution with the Preamble which every schoolboy of the "Several States" knows by heart. There was no debate on it. The delegates probably were mightily pleased with it, as Gouverneur Morris, who is responsible for the style of the instrument, was an accomplished litterateur and made of the Constitution a piece of literature, just as Thomas Jefferson did with the Declaration of Independence. But the Preamble betrays not merely the hand of the stylist. It met and overcame a serious and embarrassing difficulty. The original draft of August 6th, and the otherwise amended draft as submitted to the Committee on Style and Arrangement, spoke in the name and in behalf of the people of the States, enumerated in their geographical order from north to south, beginning with New Hampshire and ending with Georgia. The headstrong little commonwealth of Rhode Island and Providence Plantations was included, in spite of the fact that it had not sent delegates to the Convention and might not ratify the Constitution. Fortunately, this difficulty became immaterial for the purposes

Difficulty overcome in Preamble.

of the Preamble by the simple expedient of insert-
ing the word "United" before "States" and
omitting the names of the States from the balance,
so that instead of reading, "We, the people of the
States of New Hampshire", etc., the Constitution as amended would read, "We, the people
of the United States." A difficulty of a not dis-
similar kind had presented itself in the early
days of the Convention to which the reader's
attention has already been called and had been
solved in much the same way. The Virginian
plan had proposed a national legislature, a
national executive and a national judiciary, and
the Committee of the Whole reported to the Convention, under date of June 13th, its opinion that
"a national Governm⸱ ought to be established,
consisting of supreme Legislative, Executive &
Judiciary."[1] A week later, on June 20th, Mr.
Ellsworth of Connecticut, seconded by Mr. Gorham of Massachusetts, moved to alter it so as to
run "that the Government of the United States
ought to consist of a supreme Legislative, Executive and Judiciary." In behalf of his motion,
which commended itself to the Convention, as
it was unanimously adopted, he said, as reported
by Mr. Madison, that it "would drop the word
national and retain the proper title of 'The
United States.'"[2]

The Committee on Style and Arrangement,
apparently agreeing with Mr. Ellsworth, whose

[1] *Documentary History of the Constitution,* vol. iii., p. 120.
[2] *Documentary History of the Constitution,* vol. iii., p. 166.

colleague Dr. Johnson, likewise of Connecticut, was Chairman of the committee, also thought the title to be the "United States," and so thinking substituted it in lieu of the names of the thirteen. This happy modification made the Preamble ample, even although the thirteen original States should sprout like Jesse's staff. This conjecture, for the matter was apparently too trifling to be mentioned by Mr. Madison, by any member of the committee, or by any delegate to the conference, is substantiated by Mr. Chief Justice Marshall, who regarded the American people as acting in States, not as "compounded into one common mass"; and he even went so far as to say in his judicial masterpiece, what indeed one must be very sure of himself to say, that "no political dreamer was ever wild enough to think of breaking down the lines which separate the States."

Lines between the States

But whatever the true explanation of the change of phraseology may be, the Preamble is in other respects a flourish of the pen, and conveys no power to the "United States" which is not embodied in express or implied terms in the granting clauses of the Constitution. We do not need, as in the above case, to resort to conjecture, inasmuch as Mr. Justice Harlan, an advocate of "consolidation," to use the expression with which Mr. Madison and his contemporaries were familiar, said for the Supreme Court of the United States, in the case of *Jacobson* v. *Massachusetts* (197 U. S. 11,227), decided in 1905.

Although that Preamble indicates the general purposes for which the people ordained and established the Constitution, it has never been regarded as the source of any substantive power conferred on the Government of the United States or on any of its Departments. Such powers embrace only those expressly granted in the body of the Constitution and such as may be implied from those so granted. Although, therefore, one of the declared objects of the Constitution was to secure the blessings of liberty to all under the sovereign jurisdiction and authority of the United States, no power can be exerted to that end by the United States unless, apart from the Preamble, it be found in some express delegation of power or in some power to be properly implied therefrom.

THE AMERICAN UNION INTERPRETED BY THE SUPREME COURT

In the case of *Martin* v. *Hunter* (1 Wheaton, 304, 329), decided in 1816, Mr. Justice Story felt called upon to consider the origin, the nature, and the purpose of the Constitution, and, speaking for the court, he declared in language that can neither be paraphrased nor improved:

Object of the Constitution.

The object of the constitution was to establish three great departments of government; the legislative, the executive, and the judicial departments. The first was to pass laws, the second, to approve and execute them, and the third to expound and enforce them.

Admitting that Mr. Justice Story's statement is correct, of the object which the framers of the Constitution had in mind, the result can in like manner best be expressed in the language of the Supreme Court, for that tribunal has the final word in defining, construing and applying the Constitution of the United States. Of the many statements of a like nature in which the reports of the Supreme Court abound, the following, running over more than a century, can be taken as representing the views of that august tribunal from the organization of the government under the Constitution to the present day.

Thus, Mr. Justice Iredell said, in *Chisholm* v. *Georgia* (2 Dallas, 419, 435), decided in 1793:

Every State in the *Union,* in every instance where its sovereignty has not been delegated to the *United States,* I consider to be as compleatly sovereign, as the *United States* are in respect to the powers surrendered. The *United States* are sovereign as to all the powers of Government actually surrendered: Each State in the *Union* is sovereign as to all the powers reserved. It must necessarily be so, because the *United States* have no claim to any authority but such *as the States have surrendered to them:* Of course the part not surrendered must remain as it did before.

Mr. Justice Story further said, in the case of *Martin* v. *Hunter* (1 Wheaton, 304, 325-326), decided in 1816:

On the other hand, it is perfectly clear that the sovereign powers vested in the state governments, by their respective constitutions, remained unaltered and unimpaired, except so far as they were granted to the government of the United States.

These deductions do not rest upon general reasoning, plain and obvious as they seem to be. They have been positively recognised by one of the articles in amendment of the constitution, which declares, that " the powers not delegated to the United States by the constitution, nor prohibited by it to the states, are reserved to the *states* respectively, or *to the people."*

The government, then, of the United States can claim no powers which are not granted to it by the constitution, and the powers actually granted, must be such as are expressly given, or given by necessary implication.

Mr. Chief Justice Marshall, in delivering the unanimous opinion of the court over which he presided, observed in the case of *McCulloch* v. *Maryland* (4 Wheaton, 316, 410), decided in 1819, that:

In America, the powers of sovereignty are divided between the government of the Union, and those of the States. They are each sovereign, with respect to the objects committed to it, and neither sovereign with respect to the objects committed to the other.

Mr. Chief Justice Chase, upon whose sturdy shoulders the mantle of the great Chief Justice fell, impressively stated, speaking for the court in the case of *Texas* v. *White* (7 Wallace, 700, 725), decided in 1868:

Under the Articles of Confederation each State retained its sovereignty, freedom, and independence, and every power, jurisdiction, and right not expressly delegated to the United States. Under the Constitution, though the powers of the States were much restricted, still, all powers not delegated to the United States, nor prohibited to the States, are reserved to the States respectively, or to the people. And we have already had occasion to remark at this term, that "the people of each State compose a State, having its own government, and endowed with all the functions essential to separate and independent existence," and that "without the States in union, there could be no such political body as the United States." Not only, therefore, can there be no loss of separate and independent autonomy to the States, through their union under the Constitution, but it may be not unreasonably said that the preservation of the States, and the maintenance of their governments, are as much within the design and care of the Constitution as the preservation of the Union and the maintenance of the National government. The Constitution, in all its provisions, looks to an indestructible Union, composed of indestructible States.

Mr. Justice Nelson held, in the case of *Collector* v. *Day* (11 Wallace, 113, 124), decided two years later, that:

The general government, and the States, although both exist within the same territorial limits, are separate and distinct sovereignties, acting separately and independently of each other, within their respective spheres. The former in its appropriate sphere is supreme; but the States within the limits of their powers not granted, or, in the language of the tenth amendment, " re- served," are as independent of the general gov- ernment as that government within its sphere is independent of the States.

And finally, Mr. Justice Brewer, speaking for the court in the case of *South Carolina* v. *United States* (199 U. S. 437, 448), decided in 1905, thus summed up the results of a century of judicial opinion on the relation of the Union to the States and the rôle of a judiciary in the American sys- tem:

We have in this Republic a dual system of gov- ernment, National and state, each operating within the same territory and upon the same per- sons; and yet working without collision, because their functions are different. There are certain matters over which the National Government has absolute control and no action of the States can interfere therewith, and there are others in which the State is supreme, and in respect to them the. National Government is powerless. To preserve the even balance between these two governments and hold each in its separate sphere is the peculiar duty of all courts, preëminently of this —a duty oftentimes of great delicacy and diffi- culty.

IN CONCLUSION

The men meeting in conference in Philadelphia in the summer of 1787, acting under general instructions—for they could not hope to receive specific instructions on the many and vexed questions which confronted them from day to day— faced indeed a more colossal task than they themselves knew, for they not only made a Constitution for twelve States but one which meets the needs of a larger union than they could have anticipated. This Union, composed today of forty-eight States, equals in number the membership of the Society of Nations; and the official delegates of twelve of the sovereign, free and independent States of America met and solved in their conference the problems with which the official delegates of the States composing the Society of Nations will be confronted when one day their official delegates meet in conference and resolve themselves into a Committee on the State of the Society.

The framers of the Constitution recognized that they should only hope to form a Union for limited purposes and that the Government of this Union could only consist of enumerated powers. They created a legislature, not to pass statutes without let or hindrance, but to legislate upon the subjects enumerated in the grant of legislative power and to pass such laws as might be necessary or proper under the grant of power and of powers contained in the Constitution. They created an executive to carry into effect the laws thus passed in pursuance of the legislative grant, to exercise the rights and to perform the duties appertaining to his office. They created a judiciary to interpret the Constitution, to keep each government within its proper sphere, thus preventing a collision between the different branches, and confining the Union of limited powers and the States with their reserved powers within their appropriate spheres. They made the Constitution of the United States the law of the Union and of each State, so successfully indeed that the right and the duty of each can be and is fixed by judicial decision. To do this they had to define and to separate general from particular or local interests, vesting the Union with the former and leaving the latter with the States. They had to overcome the interests of the sections, which were, in some cases, so opposed as to be irreconcilable, for freedom on the one hand and slavery on the other could not be reconciled permanently.

They were met on the very threshold of the conference itself with the conflict between the large and the small States, and they settled it in the closing days of the Convention to the satisfaction of the contending parties. They did not, indeed, have all the difficulties of language, of race, of religion or traditions confronting larger international conferences, but more than one language was then and is now spoken on the

Atlantic seaboard, and the colonists were drawn from many countries and from different races. Religions were as various then as now, and the traditions were not the traditions of any one country. These differences, had they existed in a very marked degree, would have made the solution more difficult but not insurmountable to men of good will intent on a union of their States for general purposes. The experience of Switzerland, extending over many centuries, where all of these problems have presented themselves, and where they have been overcome to such a degree that the Switzerland of today has maintained its neutrality completely surrounded by belligerents of the very nationalities of which their Confederation is formed, has amply shown the accuracy of this observation.

The members of the Federal Convention were well aware that the labor of their hands might be rejected by the Conventions of the several States to which the Constitution was to be referred for ratification, and this fear is evidenced by the last resolution adopted in the last session of the Convention; that the President " retain the Journal and other papers, subject to the order of Congress, if ever formed under the Constitution."

The Constitution was a completed instrument, and lacked only the signatures of the delegates **The Ris-** approving it. " Whilst the last members were **ing Sun.** signing it," Mr. Madison says, " Doct? Franklin looking towards the President's Chair, at the

Keres, subject to the order of the Congress, if ever found under the Constitution. The members then proceeded to sign the instrument.

Whilst the members were signing ~~the Constitution~~ Doctr Franklin looking towards the Presidents Chair, at the back of which a rising sun happened to be painted, observed to a few members near him, that ~~Painters had found~~ it difficult to distinguish in their art a rising from a setting sun. I have said he, often and often in the course of the session, and the vicissitudes of my hopes and fears as to its ~~issue~~, looked at that behind the President without being able to ~~tell~~ whether it was rising or setting: But now at length I have the happiness to know that it is a rising and not a setting sun.

~~The members at the signing of the~~ The Constitution being signed by all the members except Mr. Randolph. Mr. Mason. and Mr. Gerry who declined giving it the sanction of their names, the Convention ~~dissolved themselves by an~~ Adjournment sine die —

The few alterations and corrections made in these debates which are not in my own hand writing, were dictated by me and made in my presence by John C. Payne

James Madison

M 1787

Monday May 14. was the day fixed for the meeting of the deputies in Convention for revising the federal system of Government on that day a small number only assembled.

Seven States were not convened till,

see note A. Friday 25 of May when the following members appeared

Mr. Robert Morris informed the members assembled that by the instruction & in behalf of the deputation of Penna he proposed the George Washington Esqr. for president of the Convention. Mr. Jno. Rutledge seconded the motion; expressing his confidence that the choice would be unanimous, and observing that the presence of Genl. Washington forbade any observations on the occasion which might otherwise be proper.

Washington

The General was accordingly unanimously elected by ballot. and conducted to the chair by Mr. R. Morris and Mr. Rutledge; from which in a very emphatical manner he thanked the Convention for the honor they had conferred on him, reminded them of the novelty of the scene of business in which he was to act, lamented his want of the qualifications &c and claimed the indulgence of the House towards the involuntary errors which his inexperience might occasion.

[the nomination came with particular grace from Penna, as Mr Franklin alone could have been thought of as a competitor. The Doct was himself to have made the nomination of General Washington, but the state of the weather and the state of his health confined him to his house.]

Mr. Wilson moved that a Secretary be appointed, and nominated Mr. Temple Franklin.

Col Hamilton nominated Major Jackson.

On the ballot Major Jackson had 5 votes & Mr Franklin 2 votes.

C Pinkney, in the nation of Mr. Pinkney to prepare order, was the only ...

back of which a rising sun happened to be painted, observed to a few members near him, that Painters had found it difficult to distinguish in their art a rising from a setting sun. " I have," said he, " often and often in the course of the Session, and the vicissitudes of my hopes and fears as to its issue, looked at that behind the President without being able to tell whether it was rising or setting: But now at length I have the happiness to know that it is a rising and not a setting Sun."

It is still a rising sun.

The imperfect union under the Articles gave way to the more perfect union of the Constitution, just as the imperfect union of the Society of Nations may give way to a more perfect association devised in a conference of nations, just as in the case of the American States. More than a beginning has been made. A Society of Nations is not a theory, it is a fact stated in unmistakable terms in the preamble to the Pacific Settlement Convention, drafted in 1899 by the official delegates of twenty-six States meeting in conference and acting under instructions. This Convention declared their governments as:

The Convention for the Pacific Settlement of International Disputes.

Animated by a strong desire to concert for the maintenance of the general peace;

Resolved to second by their best efforts the friendly settlement of international disputes;

Recognizing the solidarity which unites the members of the society of civilized nations;

Desirous of extending the empire of law and

of strengthening the appreciation of international justice;

Convinced that the permanent institution of a Court of Arbitration, accessible to all, in the midst of the independent Powers, will contribute effectively to this result;

Having regard to the advantages attending the general and regular organization of arbitral procedure;

Sharing the opinion of the august initiator of the International Peace Conference that it is expedient to record in an international agreement the principles of equity and right on which are based the security of States and the welfare of peoples.

That the nations of Europe could be drawn into closer relations and that the experience of the United States might serve as a precedent for such an interesting event, was foreseen, and the process stated, by Dr. Franklin in a letter which he wrote to a correspondent in Europe under date of October 22, 1787:

Benjamin Franklin's forecast.

I send you enclos'd the propos'd new Federal Constitution for these States. I was engag'd 4 Months of the last Summer in the Convention that form'd it. It is now sent by Congress to the several States for their Confirmation. If it succeeds, I do not see why you might not in Europe carry the Project of good Henry the 4th into Execution, by forming a Federal Union and One Grand Republick of all its different States & Kingdoms; by means of a like Convention; for we had many interests to reconcile.[1]

[1] Benjamin Franklin to Mr. Grand, October 22, 1787 (*Documentary History of the Constitution,* vol. iv., pp. 341-342).

The Constitution of the more perfect Union
has succeeded, and if different States and kingdoms should be inclined to substitute the regu- Madison
lated interdependence of States for their unregu- and the
liberty of
lated independence they need only turn for light the world.
and leading to the little man of Montpelier, who
has preserved for all time an exact account of
what took place in the conference of the States
in Philadelphia in the summer of 1787. Although
" the drudgery " of the undertaking " almost
killed him," it is fortunately a fact that, " by an
authentic exhibition of the objects, the opinions
and the reasonings from which the new system of
government was to receive its peculiar structure
and organization," we are now aware, as Mr.
Madison then was, " of the value of such a contribution to the fund of materials for the history of
the Constitution, on which would be staked the
happiness of a young people, great even in its
infancy and possibly the cause of liberty throughout the world."

APPENDIX

THE DECLARATION OF INDEPENDENCE—
1776 [1]

In Congress, July 4, 1776

The unanimous Declaration of the thirteen united States of America

WHEN, in the Course of human events, it becomes necessary for one people to dissolve the political bands which have connected them with another, and to assume among the Powers of the earth, the separate and equal station to which the Laws of Nature and of Nature's God entitle them, a decent respect to the opinions of mankind requires that they should declare the causes which impel them to the separation.

We hold these truths to be self-evident, that all men are created equal, that they are endowed by their Creator with certain unalienable Rights, that among these are Life, Liberty and the pursuit of Happiness. That to secure these rights, Governments are instituted among Men, deriving their just powers from the consent of the governed, That whenever any Form of Government becomes destructive of these ends, it is the Right of the People to alter or abolish it, and to institute new Government, laying its foundation on such principles and organizing its powers in such form, as to them shall seem most likely to effect their Safety and Happiness. Prudence, indeed, will dictate that Governments long established should not be changed for light and transient causes; and accordingly all experience hath shown, that mankind are more disposed to

[1] Revised Statutes of the United States, 1878, pp. 3-6.

suffer, while evils are sufferable, than to right themselves by abolishing the forms to which they are accustomed. But when a long train of abuses and usurpations, pursuing invariably the same Object evinces a design to reduce them under absolute Despotism, it is their right, it is their duty, to throw off such Government, and to provide new Guards for their future security.—Such has been the patient sufferance of these Colonies; and such is now the necessity which constrains them to alter their former Systems of Government. The history of the present King of Great Britain is a history of repeated injuries and usurpations, all having in direct object the establishment of an absolute Tyranny over these States. To prove this, let Facts be submitted to a candid world.

He has refused his Assent to Laws, the most wholesome and necessary for the public good.

He has forbidden his Governors to pass Laws of immediate and pressing importance, unless suspended in their operation till his Assent should be obtained; and when so suspended, he has utterly neglected to attend to them.

He has refused to pass other Laws for the accommodation of large districts of people, unless those people would relinquish the right of Representation in the Legislature, a right inestimable to them and formidable to tyrants only.

He has called together legislative bodies at places unusual, uncomfortable, and distant from the depository of their Public Records, for the sole purpose of fatiguing them into compliance with his measures.

He has dissolved Representative Houses repeatedly, for opposing with manly firmness his invasions on the rights of the people.

He has refused for a long time, after such dissolutions, to cause others to be elected; whereby the Legislative Powers, incapable of Annihilation, have returned to the People at large for their exercise; the State remaining in the mean time exposed to all the dangers of invasion from without, and convulsions within.

He has endeavoured to prevent the population of these States; for that purpose obstructing the Laws for Naturalization of Foreigners; refusing to pass others to encourage their migration hither, and raising the conditions of new Appropriations of Lands.

He has obstructed the Administration of Justice, by refusing his Assent to Laws for establishing Judiciary Powers.

He has made Judges dependent on his Will alone, for the tenure of their offices, and the amount and payment of their salaries.

He has erected a multitude of New Offices, and sent hither swarms of Officers to harass our People, and eat out their substance.

He has kept among us, in times of peace, Standing Armies without the consent of our legislature.

He has affected to render the Military independent of and superior to the Civil Power.

He has combined with others to subject us to a jurisdiction foreign to our constitution, and unacknowledged by our laws; giving his Assent to their acts of pretended Legislation:

For quartering large bodies of armed troops among us:

For protecting them, by a mock Trial, from Punishment for any Murders which they should commit on the Inhabitants of these States:

For cutting off our Trade with all parts of the world:

For imposing taxes on us without our Consent:

For depriving us, in many cases, of the benefits of Trial by Jury:

For transporting us beyond Seas to be tried for pretended offences:

For abolishing the free System of English Laws in a neighbouring Province, establishing therein an Arbitrary government, and enlarging its Boundaries so as to render it at once an example and fit instrument for introducing the same absolute rule into these Colonies:

For taking away our Charters, abolishing our most valuable Laws, and altering fundamentally the Forms of our Governments:

For suspending our own Legislatures, and declaring themselves invested with Power to legislate for us in all cases whatsoever.

He has abdicated Government here, by declaring us out of his Protection and waging War against us.

He has plundered our seas, ravaged our Coasts, burnt our towns, and destroyed the lives of our people.

He is at this time transporting large armies of foreign mercenaries to compleat the works of death, desolation and tyranny, already begun with circumstances of Cruelty & perfidy scarcely paralleled in the most barbarous ages, and totally unworthy the Head of a civilized nation.

He has constrained our fellow Citizens taken Captive on the high Seas to bear Arms against their Country, to become the executioners of their friends and Brethren, or to fall themselves by their Hands.

He has excited domestic insurrections amongst us, and has endeavoured to bring on the inhabitants of our frontiers, the merciless Indian Savages, whose known rule of warfare, is an undistinguished destruction of all ages, sexes and conditions.

In every stage of these Oppressions We have Petitioned for Redress in the most humble terms: Our repeated Petitions have been answered only by repeated injury. A Prince, whose character is thus marked by every act which may define a Tyrant, is unfit to be the ruler of a free People.

Nor have We been wanting in attention to our British brethren. We have warned them from time to time of attempts by their legislature to extend an unwarrantable jurisdiction over us. We have reminded them of the circumstances of our emigration and settlement here. We have appealed to their native justice and magnanimity, and we have conjured them by the ties of our common kindred to disavow these usurpations, which would inevitably interrupt our connections and correspondence. They too have been deaf to the voice of justice and of consanguinity. We must, therefore, acquiesce in the necessity, which denounces our Separation, and hold them, as we hold the rest of mankind, Enemies in War, in Peace Friends.

We, therefore, the Representatives of the united States of America, in General Congress, Assembled, appealing to the Supreme Judge of the world for the rectitude of our intentions, do, in the Name, and by Authority of the good People of these Colonies, solemnly publish and declare, That these United Colonies are, and of Right ought to be Free and Independent States; that they are Absolved from all Allegiance to the British Crown, and that all political connection between them and the State of Great Britain, is and ought to be totally dissolved; and that as Free and

Independent States, they have full Power to levy War, conclude Peace, contract Alliances, establish Commerce, and to do all other Acts and Things which Independent States may of right do. And for the support of this Declaration, with a firm reliance on the Protection of Divine Providence, we mutually pledge to each other our Lives, our Fortunes and our sacred Honor.

JOHN HANCOCK.

New Hampshire

JOSIAH BARTLETT   MATTHEW THORNTON
WM. WHIPPLE

Massachusetts Bay

SAML. ADAMS   ROBT. TREAT PAINE
JOHN ADAMS   ELBRIDGE GERRY

Rhode Island

STEP. HOPKINS   WILLIAM ELLERY

Connecticut

ROGER SHERMAN   WM. WILLIAMS
SAM'EL HUNTINGTON   OLIVER WOLCOTT

New York

WM. FLOYD   FRANS. LEWIS
PHIL. LIVINGSTON   LEWIS MORRIS

New Jersey

RICHD. STOCKTON   JOHN HART
JNO. WITHERSPOON   ABRA. CLARK
FRAS. HOPKINSON

Pennsylvania

ROBT. MORRIS · · · · · · JAS. SMITH
BENJAMIN RUSH · · · · · GEO. TAYLOR
BENJA. FRANKLIN · · · · JAMES WILSON
JOHN MORTON · · · · · · GEO. ROSS
GEO. CLYMER

Delaware

CAESAR RODNEY · · · · · THO. M'KEAN
GEO. READ

Maryland

SAMUEL CHASE · · · · · · THOS. STONE
WM. PACA · · · · · · · · · CHARLES CARROLL OF
· · · · · · · · · · · · · · · · · CARROLLTON

Virginia

GEORGE WYTHE · · · · · THOS. NELSON, JR.
RICHARD HENRY LEE · · FRANCIS LIGHTFOOT LEE
TH. JEFFERSON · · · · · · CARTER BRAXTON
BENJA. HARRISON

North Carolina

WM. HOOPER · · · · · · · JOHN PENN
JOSEPH HEWES

South Carolina

EDWARD RUTLEDGE · · · THOMAS LYNCH, Junr.
THOS. HEYWARD, Junr. · ARTHUR MIDDLETON

Georgia

BUTTON GWINNETT · · · GEO. WALTON
LYMAN HALL

ARTICLES OF CONFEDERATION—1777[1]

To all to Whom these Presents shall come, we the undersigned Delegates of the States affixed to our Names send greeting.

Whereas the Delegates of the United States of America in Congress assembled did on the fifteenth day of November in the Year of our Lord One Thousand Seven Hundred and Seventy-seven, and in the Second Year of the Independence of America agree to certain articles of Confederation and perpetual Union between the States of Newhampshire, Massachusetts-Bay, Rhodeisland and Providence Plantations, Connecticut, New York, New Jersey, Pennsylvania, Delaware, Maryland, Virginia, North-Carolina, South-Carolina and Georgia in the Words following, viz.

" Articles of Confederation and perpetual Union between the States of Newhampshire, Massachusetts-bay, Rhodeisland and Providence Plantations, Connecticut, New-York, New-Jersey, Pennsylvania, Delaware, Maryland, Virginia, North-Carolina, South-Carolina and Georgia.

ARTICLE I. THE stile of this confederacy shall be " The United States of America."

ARTICLE II. Each State retains its sovereignty, freedom and independence, and every power, jurisdiction and right, which is not by the confederation expressly delegated to the United States, in Congress assembled.

[1] Revised Statutes of the United States, pp. 7-12.

ARTICLE III. The said States hereby severally enter into a firm league of friendship with each other, for their common defence, the security of their liberties, and their mutual and general welfare, binding themselves to assist each other, against all force offered to, or attacks made upon them, or any of them, on account of religion, sovereignty, trade, or any other pretence whatever.

ARTICLE IV. The better to secure and perpetuate mutual friendship and intercourse among the people of the different States in this Union, the free inhabitants of each of these States, paupers, vagabonds and fugitives from justice excepted, shall be entitled to all privileges and immunities of free citizens in the several States; and the people of each State shall have free ingress and regress to and from any other State, and shall enjoy therein all the privileges of trade and commerce, subject to the same duties, impositions and restrictions as the inhabitants thereof respectively, provided that such restrictions shall not extend so far as to prevent the removal of property imported into any State, to any other State of which the owner is an inhabitant; provided also that no imposition, duties or restriction shall be laid by any State, on the property of the United States, or either of them.

If any person guilty of, or charged with treason, felony, or other high misdemeanor in any State, shall flee from justice, and be found in any of the United States, he shall upon demand of the Governor or Executive power, of the State from which he fled, be delivered up and removed to the State having jurisdiction of his offence.

Full faith and credit shall be given in each of these States to the records, acts and judicial proceedings of the courts and magistrates of every other State.

ARTICLE V. For the more convenient management of the general interest of the United States, delegates shall be annually appointed in such manner as the legislature of each State shall direct, to meet in Congress on the first Monday in November, in every year, with a power reserved to each State, to recall its delegates, or any of them, at any time within the year, and to send others in their stead, for the remainder of the year.

No State shall be represented in Congress by less than two, nor by more than seven members; and no person shall be capable of being a delegate for more than three years in any term of six years; nor shall any person, being a delegate, be capable of holding any office under the United States, for which he, or another for his benefit receives any salary, fees or emolument of any kind.

Each State shall maintain its own delegates in a meeting of the States, and while they act as members of the committee of the States.

In determining questions in the United States, in Congress assembled, each State shall have one vote.

Freedom of speech and debate in Congress shall not be impeached or questioned in any court, or place out of Congress, and the members of Congress shall be protected in their persons from arrests and imprisonments, during the time of their going to and from, and attendance on Congress, except for treason, felony, or breach of the peace.

ARTICLE VI. No State without the consent of the United States in Congress assembled, shall send any embassy to, or receive any embassy from, or enter into any conference, agreement, alliance or treaty with any king, prince or state; nor shall any person holding any office of profit or trust under the United States, or any of them, accept of any present, emolument, office or title of any kind whatever from any king, prince or foreign state; nor shall the United States in Congress assembled, or any of them, grant any title of nobility.

No two or more States shall enter into any treaty, confederation or alliance whatever between them, without the consent of the United States in Congress assembled, specifying accurately the purposes for which the same is to be entered into, and how long it shall continue.

No State shall lay any imposts or duties, which may interfere with any stipulations in treaties, entered into by the United States in Congress assembled, with any king, prince or state, in pursuance of any treaties already proposed by Congress, to the courts of France and Spain.

No vessels of war shall be kept up in time of peace by any State, except such number only, as shall be deemed necessary by the United States in Congress assembled, for the defence of such State, or its trade; nor shall any body of forces be kept up by any State, in time of peace, except such number only, as in the judgment of the United States, in Congress assembled, shall be deemed requisite to garrison the forts necessary for the defence of such State; but every State shall always keep up a well regulated and disciplined militia, sufficiently armed and accoutred, and shall provide and constantly have ready for use, in public stores, a due number of field pieces and tents, and a proper quantity of arms, ammunition and camp equipage.

No State shall engage in any war without the consent of the United States in Congress assembled, un-less such State be actually invaded by enemies, or shall have received certain advice of a resolution being formed by some nation of Indians to invade such State, and the danger is so imminent as not to admit of a delay, till the United States in Congress assembled can be consulted: nor shall any State grant commissions to any ships or vessels of war, nor letters of marque or reprisal, except it be after a declaration of war by the United States in Congress assembled, and then only against the kingdom or state and the subjects thereof, against which war has been so declared, and under such regulations as shall be established by the United States in Congress assembled, unless such State be infested by pirates, in which case vessels of war may be fitted out for that occasion, and kept so long as the danger shall continue, or until the United States in Congress assembled shall determine otherwise.

ARTICLE VII. When land-forces are raised by any State for the common defence, all officers of or under the rank of colonel, shall be appointed by the Legislature of each State respectively by whom such forces shall be raised, or in such manner as such State shall direct, and all vacancies shall be filled up by the State which first made the appointment.

ARTICLE VIII. All charges of war, and all other expenses that shall be incurred for the common defence or general welfare, and allowed by the United States in Congress assembled, shall be defrayed out of a common treasury, which shall be supplied by the several States, in proportion to the value of all land within each State, granted to or surveyed for any person, as such land and the buildings and improvements thereon shall be estimated according to such mode as the United States in Congress assembled, shall from time to time direct and appoint.

The taxes for paying that proportion shall be laid and levied by the authority and direction of the Legislatures of the several States within the time agreed upon by the United States in Congress assembled.

ARTICLE IX. The United States in Congress assembled, shall have the sole and exclusive right and power of determining on peace and war, except in the cases mentioned in the sixth article—of sending and receiving ambassadors—entering into treaties and alliances, provided that no treaty of commerce shall be made whereby the legislative power of the respective States shall be restrained from imposing such imposts and duties on foreigners, as their own people are subjected to, or from prohibiting the exportation or importation of any species of goods or commodities whatsoever—of establishing rules for deciding in all cases, what captures on land or water shall be legal, and in what manner prizes taken by land or naval forces in the service of the United States shall be divided or appropriated—of granting letters of marque and reprisal in times of peace—appointing courts for the trial of piracies and felonies committed on the high seas and establishing courts for receiving and determining finally appeals in all cases of captures, provided that no member of Congress shall be appointed a judge of any of the said courts.

The United States in Congress assembled shall also be the last resort on appeal in all disputes and differences now subsisting or that hereafter may arise between two or more States concerning boundary, jurisdiction or any other cause whatever; which authority shall always be exercised in the manner following.

Whenever the legislative or executive authority or lawful agent of any State in controversy with another shall present a petition to Congress, stating the matter in question and praying for a hearing, notice thereof shall be given by order of Congress to the legislative or executive authority of the other State in controversy, and a day assigned for the appearance of the parties by their lawful agents, who shall then be directed to appoint by joint consent, commissioners or judges to constitute a court for hearing and determining the matter in question: but if they can not agree, Congress shall name three persons out of each of the United States, and from the list of such persons each party shall alternately strike out one, the petitioners beginning, until the number shall be reduced to thirteen; and from that number not less than seven, nor more than nine names as Congress shall direct, shall in the presence of Congress be drawn out by lot, and the persons whose names shall be so drawn or any five of them, shall be commissioners or judges, to hear and finally determine the controversy, so always as a major part of the judges who shall hear the cause shall agree in the determination: and if either party shall neglect to attend at the day appointed, without showing reasons, which Congress shall judge sufficient, or being present shall refuse to strike, the Congress shall proceed to nominate three persons out of each State, and the Secretary of Congress shall strike in behalf of such party absent or refusing; and the judgment and sentence of the court to be appointed, in the manner before prescribed, shall be final and conclusive; and if any of the parties shall refuse to submit to the authority of such court, or to appear or defend their claim or cause, the court shall nevertheless proceed to pronounce sentence, or judgment, which shall in like manner be final and decisive, the judgment or sentence and other proceedings being in either case transmitted to Congress, and lodged among the acts of Congress for the security of the parties concerned: provided that every commissioner, before he sits in judgment, shall take an oath to be administered by one of the judges of the supreme or superior court of the State, where the cause shall be tried, " well and truly to hear and determine the matter in question, according to the best of his judgment, without favour, affection or hope of reward:" provided also that no State shall be deprived of territory for the benefit of the United States.

All controversies concerning the private right of soil claimed under different grants of two or more States, whose jurisdiction as they may respect such lands, and the States which passed such grants are adjusted, the said grants or either of them being at the same time claimed to have originated antecedent to such settlement of jurisdiction, shall on the petition of either party to the Congress of the United States, be finally determined as near as may be in the same manner as is before prescribed for deciding disputes respecting territorial jurisdiction between different States.

The United States in Congress assembled shall also have the sole and exclusive right and power of regulating the alloy and value of coin struck by their own authority, or by that of the respective States,—fixing the standard of weights and measures throughout the United States,—regulating the trade and managing all affairs with the Indians, not members of any of the States, provided that the legislative right of any State within its own limits be not infringed or violated— establishing and regulating post-offices from one State to another, throughout all the United States, and exacting such postage on the papers passing thro' the same as may be requisite to defray the expenses of the said office—appointing all officers of the land forces, in the service of the United States, excepting regimental offiers—appointing all the officers of the naval forces, and commissioning all officers whatever in the service of the United States—making rules for the government and regulation of the said land and naval forces, and directing their operations.

The United States in Congress assembled shall have authority to appoint a committee, to sit in the recess of Congress, to be denominated "A Committee of the States," and to consist of one delegate from each State; and to appoint such other committees and civil officers as may be necessary for managing the general affairs of the United States under their direction—to appoint one of their number to preside, provided that no person be allowed to serve in the office of president more than one year in any term of three years; to ascertain the necessary sums of money to be raised for the service of the United States, and to appropriate and apply the same for defraying the public expenses—to borrow money, or emit bills on the credit of the United States, transmitting every half year to the respective States an account of the sums of money so borrowed or emitted, —to build and equip a navy—to agree upon the number of land forces, and to make requisitions from each State for its quota, in proportion to the number of white inhabitants in such State; which requisition shall be binding, and thereupon the Legislature of each State shall appoint the regimental officers, raise the men and cloath, arm and equip them in a soldier like manner, at the expense of the United States; and the officers and men so cloathed, armed and equipped shall march to the place appointed, and within the time agreed on by the United States in Congress assembled: but if the United States in Congress assembled shall, on consideration of circumstances, judge proper that any State should not raise men, or should raise a smaller number than its quota, and that any other State should raise a greater number of men than the quota thereof, such extra number shall be raised, officered, cloathed, armed and equipped in the same manner as the quota of such State, unless the legislature of such State shall judge that such extra number cannot be safely spared out of the same, in which case they shall raise, officer, cloath, arm and equip as many of such extra number as they judge can be safely spared. And the officers and men so cloathed, armed and equipped, shall march to the place appointed, and within the time agreed on by the United States in Congress assembled.

The United States in Congress assembled shall never engage in a war, nor grant letters of marque and reprisal in time of peace, nor enter into any treaties or alliances, nor coin money, nor regulate the value thereof, nor ascertain the sums and expenses necessary for the defence and welfare of the United States, or any of them, nor emit bills, nor borrow money on the credit of the United States, nor appropriate money, nor agree upon the number of vessels of war, to be built or purchased, or the number of land or sea forces to be raised, nor appoint a commander in chief of the army or navy, unless nine States assent to the same: nor shall a question on any other point, except for adjourning from day to day be determined, unless by the votes of a majority of the United States in Congress assembled.

The Congress of the United States shall have power to adjourn to any time within the year, and to any place within the United States, so that no period of adjournment be for a longer duration than the space of six months, and shall publish the journal of their proceedings monthly except such parts thereof relating to treaties, alliances or military operations, as in their judgment require secrecy; and the yeas and nays of the delegates of each State on any question shall be entered on the journal, when it is desired by any delegate; and the delegates of a State, or any of them, at his or their request shall be furnished with a transcript of the said journal, except such parts as are above excepted, to lay before the Legislatures of the several States.

ARTICLE X. The committee of the States, or any nine of them, shall be authorized to execute, in the recess of Congress, such of the powers of Congress as the United States in Congress assembled, by the consent of nine States, shall from time to time think expedient to vest them with; provided that no power be delegated to the said committee, for the exercise of which, by the articles of confederation, the voice of nine States in the Congress of the United States assembled is requisite.

ARTICLE XI. Canada acceding to this confederation, and joining in the measures of the United States, shall be admitted into, and entitled to all the advantages of this Union: but no other colony shall be admitted into the same, unless such admission be agreed to by nine States.

ARTICLE XII. All bills of credit emitted, monies

borrowed and debts contracted by, or under the authority of Congress, before the assembling of the United
States, in pursuance of the present confederation, shall
be deemed and considered as a charge against the
United States, for payment and satisfaction whereof
the said United States, and the public faith are hereby
solemnly pledged.

ARTICLE XIII. Every State shall abide by the determinations of the United States in Congress assembled, on all questions which by this confederation are
submitted to them. And the articles of this confederation shall be inviolably observed by every State,
and the Union shall be perpetual; nor shall any alteration at any time hereafter be made in any of them; unless such alteration be agreed to in a Congress of the
United States, and be afterwards confirmed by the
Legislatures of every State.

And whereas it hath pleased the Great Governor of
the world to incline the hearts of the Legislatures we
respectively represent in Congress, to approve of, and
to authorize us to ratify the said articles of confederation and perpetual union. Know ye that we the undersigned delegates, by virtue of the power and authority
to us given for that purpose, do by these presents, in
the name and in behalf of our respective constituents,
fully and entirely ratify and confirm each and every
of the said articles of confederation and perpetual
union, and all and singular the matters and things
therein contained: And we do further solemnly plight
and engage the faith of our respective constituents, that
they shall abide by the determinations of the United
States in Congress assembled, on all questions, which
by the said confederation are submitted to them. And
that the articles thereof shall be inviolably observed by

the States we re[s]pectively represent, and that the Union shall be perpetual.

In witness whereof we have hereunto set our hands in Congress. Done at Philadelphia in the State of Pennsylvania the ninth day of July in the year of our Lord one thousand seven hundred and seventy-eight, and in the third year of the independence of America.

On the part & behalf of the State of New Hampshire.

JOSIAH BARTLETT,   JOHN   WENTWORTH,
                       Junr.,
                                August 8th, 1778.

On the part and behalf of the State of Massachusetts Bay.

JOHN HANCOCK,   FRANCIS DANA,
SAMUEL ADAMS,   JAMES LOVELL,
ELBRIDGE GERRY   SAMUEL HOLTEN.

On the part and behalf of the State of Rhode Island and Providence Plantations.

WILLIAM ELLERY,   JOHN COLLINS.
HENRY MARCHANT,

On the part and behalf of the State of Connecticut.

ROGER SHERMAN,   TITUS HOSMER,
SAMUEL HUNTINGTON,   ANDREW ADAMS.
OLIVER WOLCOTT,

On the part and behalf of the State of New York.

JAS. DUANE,   WM. DUER,
FRA. LEWIS,   GOUV. MORRIS.

On the part and in behalf of the State of New Jersey, Novr. 26, 1778.

JNO. WITHERSPOON,   NATHL. SCUDDER.

On the part and behalf of the State of Pennsylvania.

ROBT. MORRIS,   WILLIAM CLINGAN,
DANIEL ROBERDEAU,   JOSEPH REED, 22d July,
JONA. BAYARD SMITH, 1778.

On the part & behalf of the State of Delaware.

THO. M'KEAN, Feby. 12, NICHOLAS VAN DYKE.
1779.
JOHN DICKINSON, May
5th, 1779.

On the part and behalf of the State of Maryland.

JOHN HANSON, March 1, DANIEL CARROLL, Mar.
1781.   1, 1781.

On the part and behalf of the State of Virginia.

RICHARD HENRY LEE,   JNO. HARVIE,
JOHN BANISTER,   FRANCIS LIGHTFOOT LEE.
THOMAS ADAMS,

On the part and behalf of the State of No. Carolina.

JOHN PENN, July 21st, CORNS. HARNETT,
1778.   JNO. WILLIAMS.

On the part and behalf of the State of South Carolina.

HENRY LAURENS,   JNO. MATTHEWS,
WILLIAM HENRY DRAY- RICHD. HUTSON,
TON,   THOS. HEYWARD, Junr.

On the part & behalf of the State of Georgia.

JNO. WALTON, 24th July, EDWD. TELFAIR,
1778.   EDWD. LANGWORTHY.

THE CONSTITUTION OF THE UNITED STATES—1787 [1]

WE THE PEOPLE of the United States, in Order to form a more perfect Union, establish Justice, insure domestic Tranquility, provide for the common defence, promote the general Welfare, and secure the Blessings of Liberty to ourselves and our Posterity, do ordain and establish this CONSTITUTION for the United States of America.

ARTICLE I.

SECTION 1. All legislative Powers herein granted shall be vested in a Congress of the United States, which shall consist of a Senate and House of Representatives.

SECTION 2. [1] The House of Representatives shall be composed of Members chosen every second Year by the People of the several States, and the Electors in each State shall have the Qualifications requisite for Electors of the most numerous Branch of the State Legislature.

[2] No Person shall be a Representative who shall not have attained the Age of twenty-five Years, and been seven Years a Citizen of the United States, and who shall not, when elected, be an Inhabitant of that State in which he shall be chosen.

[1] The text of the Constitution, and the amendments thereto, are taken from the Revised Statutes of the United States, 1878, and Senate Document No. 12, 63d Congress, 1st Session.

The numbers prefixed to the clauses of the Constitution, and here placed in parentheses, do not appear in the original text.

(3)*[Representatives and direct Taxes shall be apportioned among the several States which may be included within this Union, according to their respective Numbers, which shall be determined by adding to the whole Number of free Persons, including those bound to Service for a Term of Years, and excluding Indians not taxed, three fifths of all other Persons.] The actual Enumeration shall be made within three Years after the first Meeting of the Congress of the United States, and within every subsequent Term of ten Years, in such Manner as they shall by Law direct. The Number of Representatives shall not exceed one for every thirty Thousand, but each State shall have at Least one Representative; and until such enumeration shall be made, the State of New Hampshire shall be entitled to chuse three, Massachusetts eight, Rhode-Island and Providence Plantations one, Connecticut five, New-York six, New Jersey four, Pennsylvania eight, Delaware one, Maryland six, Virginia ten, North Carolina five, South Carolina five, and Georgia three.

(4) When vacancies happen in the Representation from any State, the Executive Authority thereof shall issue Writs of Election to fill such Vacancies.

(5) The House of Representatives shall chuse their Speaker and other Officers; and shall have the sole Power of Impeachment.

SECTION 3. [(1) The Senate of the United States shall be composed of two Senators from each State, chosen by the Legislature thereof, for six Years; and each Senator shall have one Vote.]†

* The clause included in brackets is amended by the fourteenth amendment, 2d Session.

† The first paragraph of section three of Article 1, of the Constitution of the United States, and so much of paragraph two of the same section as relates to filling vacancies are amended by the seventeenth amendment to the Constitution.

(2) Immediately after they shall be assembled in Consequence of the first Election, they shall be divided as equally as may be into three Classes. The Seats of the Senators of the first Class shall be vacated at the Expiration of the second Year, of the second Class at the Expiration of the fourth Year, and of the third Class at the Expiration of the sixth Year, so that one-third may be chosen every second Year; and if Vacancies happen by Resignation, or otherwise, during the Recess of the Legislature of any State, the Executive thereof may make temporary Appointments [until the next Meeting of the Legislature, which shall then fill such Vacancies].

(3) No Person shall be a Senator who shall not have attained to the Age of thirty Years, and been nine Years a Citizen of the United States, and who shall not, when elected, be an Inhabitant of that State for which he shall be chosen.

(4) The Vice President of the United States shall be President of the Senate, but shall have no Vote, unless they be equally divided.

(5) The Senate shall chuse their other Officers, and also a President pro tempore, in the Absence of the Vice President, or when he shall exercise the Office of President of the United States.

(6) The Senate shall have the sole Power to try all Impeachments. When sitting for that Purpose, they shall be on Oath or Affirmation. When the President of the United States is tried, the Chief Justice shall preside: And no Person shall be convicted without the Concurrence of two thirds of the Members present.

(7) Judgment in Cases of Impeachment shall not extend further than to removal from Office, and disqualification to hold and enjoy any Office of honor,

Trust or Profit under the United States: but the Party convicted shall nevertheless be liable and subject to Indictment, Trial, Judgment and Punishment, according to Law.

SECTION 4. [1] The Times, Places and Manner of holding Elections for Senators and Representatives, shall be prescribed in each State by the Legislature thereof; but the Congress may at any time by Law make or alter such Regulations, except as to the Places of chusing Senators.

[2] The Congress shall assemble at least once in every Year, and such Meeting shall be on the first Monday in December, unless they shall by Law appoint a different Day.

SECTION 5. [1] Each House shall be the Judge of the Elections, Returns and Qualifications of its own Members, and a Majority of each shall constitute a Quorum to do Business; but a smaller Number may adjourn from day to day, and may be authorized to compel the Attendance of absent Members, in such Manner, and under such Penalties as each House may provide.

[2] Each House may determine the Rules of its Proceedings, punish its Members for disorderly Behaviour, and, with the Concurrence of two thirds, expel a Member.

[3] Each House shall keep a Journal of its Proceedings, and from time to time publish the same, excepting such Parts as may in their Judgment require Secrecy; and the Yeas and Nays of the Members of either House on any question shall, at the Desire of one fifth of those Present, be entered on the Journal.

[4] Neither House, during the Session of Congress, shall, without the consent of the other, adjourn for

more than three days, nor to any other Place than that in which the two Houses shall be sitting.

SECTION 6. [1] The Senators and Representatives shall receive a Compensation for their Services, to be ascertained by Law, and paid out of the Treasury of the United States. They shall in all Cases, except Treason, Felony and Breach of the Peace, be privileged from Arrest during their Attendance at the Session of their respective Houses, and in going to and returning from the same; and for any Speech or Debate in either House, they shall not be questioned in any other Place.

[2] No Senator or Representative shall, during the Time for which he was elected, be appointed to any civil Office under the Authority of the United States, which shall have been created, or the Emoluments whereof shall have been encreased during such time; and no Person holding any Office under the United States, shall be a Member of either House during his Continuance in Office.

SECTION 7. [1] All Bills for raising Revenue shall originate in the House of Representatives; but the Senate may propose or concur with Amendments as on other Biils.

[2] Every Bill which shall have passed the House of Representatives and the Senate, shall, before it become a Law, be presented to the President of the United States; If he approve he shall sign it, but if not he shall return it, with his Objections to that House in which it shall have originated, who shall enter the Objections at large on their Journal, and proceed to reconsider it. If after such Reconsideration two thirds of that House shall agree to pass the Bill, it shall be sent, together with the Objections, to the other House, by which it

shall likewise be reconsidered, and if approved by two thirds of that House, it shall become a Law. But in all such Cases the Votes of both Houses shall be determined by Yeas and Nays, and the Names of the Persons voting for and against the Bill shall be entered on the Journal of each House respectively. If any Bill shall not be returned by the President within ten Days (Sundays excepted) after it shall have been presented to him, the Same shall be a Law, in like Manner as if he had signed it, unless the Congress by their Adjournment prevent its Return, in which Case it shall not be a Law.

[3] Every Order, Resolution, or Vote to which the Concurrence of the Senate and House of Representatives may be necessary (except on a question of Adjournment) shall be presented to the President of the United States; and before the Same shall take Effect, shall be approved by him, or being disapproved by him, shall be repassed by two thirds of the Senate and House of Representatives, according to the Rules and Limitations prescribed in the Case of a Bill.

SECTION 8. The Congress shall have Power [1] To lay and collect Taxes, Duties, Imposts and Excises, to pay the Debts and provide for the common Defence and general Welfare of the United States; but all Duties, Imposts and Excises shall be uniform throughout the United States;

[2] To borrow money on the credit of the United States;

[3] To regulate Commerce with foreign Nations, and among the several States, and with the Indian Tribes;

[4] To establish an uniform Rule of Naturalization, and uniform Laws on the subject of Bankruptcies throughout the United States;

(5) To coin Money, regulate the Value thereof, and of foreign Coin, and fix the Standard of Weights and Measures;

(6) To provide for the Punishment of counterfeiting the Securities and current Coin of the United States;

(7) To establish Post Offices and post Roads;

(8) To promote the Progress of Science and useful Arts, by securing for limited Times to Authors and Inventors the exclusive Right to their respective Writings and Discoveries;

(9) To constitute Tribunals inferior to the supreme Court;

(10) To define and punish Piracies and Felonies committed on the high Seas, and Offenses against the Law of Nations;

(11) To declare War, grant Letters of Marque and Reprisal, and make Rules concerning Captures on Land and Water;

(12) To raise and support Armies, but no Appropriation of Money to that Use shall be for a longer Term than two Years;

(13) To provide and maintain a Navy;

(14) To make Rules for the Government and Regulation of the land and naval Forces;

(15) To provide for calling forth the Militia to execute the Laws of the Union, suppress Insurrections and repel Invasions;

(16) To provide for organizing, arming, and disciplining the Militia, and for governing such Part of them as may be employed in the Service of the United States, reserving to the States respectively, the Appointment of the Officers, and the Authority of training the Militia according to the discipline prescribed by Congress;

(17) To exercise exclusive Legislation in all Cases whatsoever, over such District (not exceeding ten Miles square) as may, by Cession of particular States, and the Acceptance of Congress, become the seat of the Government of the United States, and to exercise like Authority over all Places purchased by the Consent of the Legislature of the State in which the Same shall be, for the Erection of Forts, Magazines, Arsenals, dock-Yards, and other needful Buildings;—And

(18) To make all Laws which shall be necessary and proper for carrying into Execution the foregoing Powers, and all other Powers vested by this Constitution in the Government of the United States, or in any Department or Officer thereof.

SECTION 9. (1) The Migration or Importation of such Persons as any of the States now existing shall think proper to admit, shall not be prohibited by the Congress prior to the Year one thousand eight hundred and eight, but a tax or duty may be imposed on such Importation, not exceeding ten dollars for each Person.

(2) The Privilege of the Writ of Habeas Corpus shall not be suspended, unless when in Cases of Rebellion or Invasion the public Safety may require it.

(3) No Bill of Attainder or ex post facto Law shall be passed.

*(4) No Capitation, or other direct, Tax shall be laid, unless in Proportion to the Census or Enumeration herein before directed to be taken.

(5) No Tax or Duty shall be laid on Articles exported from any State.

(6) No Preference shall be given by any Regulation of Commerce or Revenue to the Ports of one State over those of another: nor shall Vessels bound to, or

* See XVI Amendment.

from, one State, be obliged to enter, clear, or pay Duties in another.

(7) No Money shall be drawn from the Treasury, but in Consequence of Appropriations made by Law; and a regular Statement and Account of the Receipts and Expenditures of all public Money shall be published from time to time.

(8) No Title of Nobility shall be granted by the United States; and no Person holding any Office of Profit or Trust under them, shall, without the Consent of the Congress, accept of any present, Emolument, Office, or Title, of any kind whatever, from any King, Prince, or foreign State.

SECTION 10. (1) No State shall enter into any Treaty, Alliance, or Confederation; grant Letters of Marque and Reprisal; coin Money; emit Bills of Credit; make any Thing but gold and silver Coin a Tender in Payment of Debts; pass any Bill of Attainder, ex post facto Law, or Law impairing the Obligation of Contracts, or grant any Title of Nobility.

(2) No State shall, without the Consent of the Congress, lay any Imposts or Duties on Imports or Exports, except what may be absolutely necessary for executing its inspection Laws: and the net Produce of all Duties and Imposts, laid by any State on Imports or Exports, shall be for the Use of the Treasury of the United States; and all such Laws shall be subject to the Revision and Control of the Congress.

(3) No State shall, without the Consent of Congress, lay any duty of Tonnage, keep Troops, or Ships of War in time of Peace, enter into any Agreement or Compact with another State, or with a foreign Power, or engage in War, unless actually invaded, or in such imminent Danger as will not admit of delay.

ARTICLE II.

SECTION I. ⁽¹⁾ The executive Power shall be vested in a President of the United States of America. He shall hold his Office during the Term of four Years, and, together with the Vice President, chosen for the same Term, be elected, as follows:

⁽²⁾ Each State shall appoint, in such Manner as the Legislature thereof may direct, a Number of Electors, equal to the whole Number of Senators and Representatives to which the State may be entitled in the Congress: but no Senator or Representative, or Person holding an Office of Trust or Profit under the United States, shall be appointed an Elector.

*[The Electors shall meet in their respective States, and vote by Ballot for two persons, of whom one at least shall not be an Inhabitant of the same State with themselves. And they shall make a List of all the Persons voted for, and of the Number of Votes for each; which List they shall sign and certify, and transmit sealed to the Seat of the Government of the United States, directed to the President of the Senate. The President of the Senate shall, in the Presence of the Senate and House of Representatives, open all the Certificates, and the Votes shall then be counted. The Person having the greatest Number of Votes shall be the President, if such Number be a Majority of the whole Number of Electors appointed; and if there be more than one who have such Majority, and have an equal Number of Votes, then the House of Representatives shall immediately chuse by Ballot one of them for President; and if no Person have a Majority, then from the five highest on the List the said House shall in like

* This clause has been superseded by the twelfth amendment.

Manner chuse the President. But in chusing the President, the Votes shall be taken by States, the Representation from each State having one Vote; A quorum for this Purpose shall consist of a Member or Members from two thirds of the States, and a Majority of all the States shall be necessary to a Choice. In every Case, after the Choice of the President, the Person having the greatest Number of Votes of the Electors shall be the Vice President. But if there should remain two or more who have equal Votes, the Senate shall chuse from them by Ballot the Vice President.]

(3) The Congress may determine the Time of chusing the Electors, and the Day on which they shall give their Votes; which Day shall be the same throughout the United States.

(4) No Person except a natural born Citizen, or a Citizen of the United States, at the time of the Adoption of this Constitution, shall be eligible to the Office of President; neither shall any Person be eligible to that Office who shall not have attained to the Age of thirty five Years, and been fourteen Years a Resident within the United States.

(5) In Case of the Removal of the President from Office, or of his Death, Resignation, or Inability to discharge the Powers and Duties of the said Office, the Same shall devolve on the Vice President, and the Congress may by Law provide for the Case of Removal, Death, Resignation or Inability, both of the President and Vice President, declaring what Officer shall then act as President, and such Officer shall act accordingly, until the Disability be removed, or a President shall be elected.

(6) The President shall, at stated Times, receive for his Services, a Compensation, which shall neither be

encreased nor diminished during the Period for which he shall have been elected, and he shall not receive within that Period any other Emolument from the United States, or any of them.

(7) Before he enter on the Execution of his Office, he shall take the following Oath or Affirmation:—" I do solemnly swear (or affirm) that I will faithfully execute the Office of President of the United States, and will to the best of my Ability, preserve, protect and defend the Constitution of the United States."

SECTION 2. (1) The President shall be Commander in Chief of the Army and Navy of the United States, and of the Militia of the several States, when called into the actual Service of the United States; he may require the Opinion, in writing, of the principal Officer in each of the executive Departments, upon any Subject relating to the Duties of their respective Offices, and he shall have Power to grant Reprieves and Pardons for Offences against the United States, except in Cases of Impeachment.

(2) He shall have Power, by and with the Advice and Consent of the Senate, to make Treaties, provided two thirds of the Senators present concur; and he shall nominate, and by and with the Advice and Consent of the Senate, shall appoint Ambassadors, other public Ministers and Consuls, Judges of the supreme Court, and all other Officers of the United States, whose Appointments are not herein otherwise provided for, and which shall be established by Law: but the Congress may by Law vest the Appointment of such inferior Officers, as they think proper, in the President alone, in the Courts of Law, or in the Heads of Departments.

(3) The President shall have Power to fill up all Vacancies that may happen during the Recess of the

Senate, by granting Commissions which shall expire at the End of their next session.

SECTION 3. He shall from time to time give to the Congress Information of the State of the Union, and recommend to their Consideration such Measures as he shall judge necessary and expedient; he may, on extraordinary Occasions, convene both Houses, or either of them, and in Case of Disagreement between them, with Respect to the Time of Adjournment, he may adjourn them to such Time as he shall think proper; he shall receive Ambassadors and other public Ministers; he shall take Care that the Laws be faithfully executed, and shall Commission all the Officers of the United States.

SECTION 4. The President, Vice President and all civil Officers of the United States, shall be removed from Office on Impeachment for, and Conviction of, Treason, Bribery, or other high Crimes and Misdemeanors.

ARTICLE III.

SECTION I. The judicial Power of the United States, shall be vested in one supreme Court, and in such inferior Courts as the Congress may from time to time ordain and establish. The Judges, both of the supreme and inferior Courts, shall hold their Offices during good Behaviour, and shall, at Stated Times, receive for their Services, a Compensation, which shall not be diminished during their Continuance in Office.

SECTION 2. [1] The judicial Power shall extend to all Cases, in Law and Equity, arising under this Constitution, the Laws of the United States, and Treaties made, or which shall be made, under their Authority;—to all

Cases affecting Ambassadors, or other public Ministers and Consuls;—to all Cases of admiralty and maritime Jurisdiction;—to Controversies to which the United States shall be a Party;—to Controversies between two or more States;—between a State and Citizens of another State;—between Citizens of different States;—between Citizens of the same State claiming Lands under Grants of different States, and between a State, or the Citizens thereof, and foreign States, Citizens or Subjects.

(2) In all Cases affecting Ambassadors, other public Ministers and Consuls, and those in which a State shall be Party, the supreme Court shall have original Jurisdiction. In all the other Cases before mentioned, the supreme Court shall have appellate Jurisdiction, both as to Law and Fact, with such Exceptions, and under such Regulations as the Congress shall make.

(3) The Trial of all Crimes, except in Cases of Impeachment, shall be by Jury; and such Trial shall be held in the State where the said Crimes shall have been committed; but when not committed within any State, the Trial shall be at such Place or Places as the Congress may by Law have directed.

SECTION 3. (1) Treason against the United States, shall consist only in levying War against them, or in adhering to their Enemies, giving them Aid and Comfort. No Person shall be convicted of Treason unless on the Testimony of two Witnesses to the same overt Act, or on Confession in open Court.

(2) The Congress shall have Power to declare the Punishment of Treason, but no Attainder of Treason shall work Corruption of Blood, or Forfeiture except during the Life of the Person attainted.

ARTICLE IV.

SECTION 1. Full Faith and Credit shall be given in each State to the public Acts, Records, and judicial Proceedings of every other State. And the Congress may by general Laws prescribe the Manner in which such Acts, Records and Proceedings shall be proved, and the Effect thereof.

SECTION 2. [1] The Citizens of each State shall be entitled to all Privileges and Immunities of Citizens in the several States.

[2] A Person charged in any State with Treason, Felony, or other Crime, who shall flee from Justice, and be found in another State, shall on Demand of the executive Authority of the State from which he fled, be delivered up, to be removed to the State having jurisdiction of the Crime.

[3] No Person held to Service or Labour in one State, under the Laws thereof, escaping into another, shall, in Consequence of any Law or Regulation therein, be discharged from such Service or Labour, but shall be delivered up on Claim of the Party to whom such Service or Labour may be due.

SECTION 3. [1] New States may be admitted by the Congress into this Union; but no new State shall be formed or erected within the Jurisdiction of any other State; nor any State be formed by the Junction of two or more States, or Parts of States, without the Consent of the Legislatures of the States concerned as well as of the Congress.

[2] The Congress shall have Power to dispose of and make all needful Rules and Regulations respecting the Territory or other Property belonging to the United States; and nothing in this Constitution shall be so con-

strued as to Prejudice any Claims of the United States, or of any particular State.

SECTION 4. The United States shall guarantee to every State in this Union a Republican Form of Government, and shall protect each of them against Invasion; and on Application of the Legislature, or of the Executive (when the Legislature cannot be convened) against domestic Violence.

ARTICLE V.

The Congress, whenever two-thirds of both Houses shall deem it necessary, shall propose Amendments to this Constitution, or, on the Application of the Legislatures of two thirds of the several States, shall call a Convention for proposing Amendments, which, in either Case, shall be valid to all Intents and Purposes, as Part of this Constitution, when ratified by the Legislatures of three fourths of the several States, or by Conventions in three fourths thereof, as the one or the other Mode of Ratification may be proposed by the Congress; Provided that no Amendment which may be made prior to the Year One thousand eight hundred and eight shall in any Manner affect the first and fourth Clauses in the Ninth Section of the first Article; and that no State, without its Consent, shall be deprived of it's equal Suffrage in the Senate.

ARTICLE VI.

[1] All Debts contracted and Engagements entered into, before the Adoption of this Constitution, shall be as valid against the United States under this Constitution, as under the Confederation.

[2] This Constitution, and the Laws of the United

States which shall be made in Pursuance thereof; and all Treaties made, or which shall be made, under the Authority of the United States, shall be the supreme Law of the Land; and the Judges in every State shall be bound thereby, any Thing in the Constitution or Laws of any State to the Contrary notwithstanding.

[3] The Senators and Representatives before mentioned, and the Members of the several State Legislatures, and all executive and judicial Officers, both of the United States and of the several States, shall be bound by Oath or Affirmation, to support this Constitution; but no religious Test shall ever be required as a Qualification to any Office or public Trust under the United States.

ARTICLE VII.

The Ratification of the Conventions of nine States, shall be sufficient for the Establishment of this Constitution between the States so ratifying the Same.

Done in Convention by the Unanimous Consent of the States present the Seventeenth Day of September in the Year of our Lord one thousand seven hundred and Eighty seven, and of the Independence of the United States of America the Twelfth. **In Witness** whereof We have hereunto subscribed our Names.

G?: WASHINGTON
Presidt and deputy from Virginia

New Hampshire.
JOHN LANGDON   NICHOLAS GILMAN

Massachusetts.
NATHANIEL GORHAM   RUFUS KING

Connecticut.
WM. SAML. JOHNSON   ROGER SHERMAN

New York.

ALEXANDER HAMILTON

New Jersey.

WIL: LIVINGSTON   WM. PATTERSON
DAVID BREARLEY   JONA: DAYTON

Pennsylvania.

B. FRANKLIN   THOMAS MIFFLIN
ROBT. MORRIS   GEO. CLYMER
THOS. FITZSIMONS   JARED INGERSOLL
JAMES WILSON   GOUV MORRIS

Delaware.

GEO: READ   GUNNING BEDFORD Jun
JOHN DICKINSON   RICHARD BASSETT
JACO: BROOM

Maryland.

JAMES MCHENRY   DAN of ST THOS JENI-
DANL. CARROLL   FER

Virginia.

JOHN BLAIR—   JAMES MADISON Jr.

North Carolina.

WM. BLOUNT   RICHD DOBBS SPAIGHT,
HU WILLIAMSON

South Carolina.

J. RUTLEDGE   CHARLES COTESWORTH
CHARLES PINCKNEY   PINCKNEY
                         PIERCE BUTLER

Georgia.

WILLIAM FEW   ABR BALDWIN

Attest   WILLIAM JACKSON *Secretary*

ARTICLES IN ADDITION TO, AND AMENDMENT OF, THE CONSTITUTION OF THE UNITED STATES OF AMERICA, PROPOSED BY CONGRESS, AND RATIFIED BY THE LEGISLATURES OF THE SEVERAL STATES, PURSUANT TO THE FIFTH ARTICLE OF THE ORIGINAL CONSTITUTION.

[ARTICLE I.]*

Congress shall make no law respecting an establishment of religion, or prohibiting the free exercise thereof; or abridging the freedom of speech, or of the press; or the right of the people peaceably to assemble, and to petition the Government for a redress of grievances.

[ARTICLE II.]

A well regulated Militia, being necessary to the security of a free State, the right of the people to keep and bear Arms, shall not be infringed.

* The first ten amendments to the Constitution of the United States were proposed to the legislatures of the several States by the First Congress, on the 25th of September, 1789. They were ratified by the following States, and the notifications of ratification by the governors thereof were successively communicated by the President to Congress: New Jersey, November 20, 1789; Maryland, December 19, 1789; North Carolina, December 22, 1789; South Carolina, January 19, 1790; New Hampshire, January 25, 1790; Delaware, January 28, 1790; Pennsylvania, March 10, 1790; New York, March 27, 1790; Rhode Island, June 15, 1790; Vermont, November 3, 1791, and Virginia, December 15, 1791. There is no evidence on the journals of Congress that the legislatures of Connecticut, Georgia, and Massachusetts ratified them.

[ARTICLE III.]

No Soldier shall, in time of peace, be quartered in any house, without the consent of the Owner, nor in time of war, but in a manner to be prescribed by law.

[ARTICLE IV.]

The right of the people to be secure in their persons, houses, papers, and effects, against unreasonable searches and seizures, shall not be violated, and no Warrants shall issue, but upon probable cause, supported by Oath or affirmation, and particularly describing the place to be searched, and the persons or things to be seized.

[ARTICLE V.]

No person shall be held to answer for a capital, or otherwise infamous crime, unless on a presentment or indictment of a Grand Jury, except in cases arising in the land or naval forces, or in the Militia, when in actual service in time of War or public danger; nor shall any person be subject for the same offence to be twice put in jeopardy of life or limb; nor shall be compelled in any criminal case to be a witness against himself, nor be deprived of life, liberty, or property, without due process of law; nor shall private property be taken for public use, without just compensation.

[ARTICLE VI.]

In all criminal prosecutions, the accused shall enjoy the right to a speedy and public trial, by an impartial jury of the State and district wherein the crime shall have been committed, which district shall have been previously ascertained by law, and to be informed of

144 Madison's Debates in Federal Convention

the nature and cause of the accusation; to be confronted with the witnesses against him; to have compulsory process for obtaining witnesses in his favor, and to have the Assistance of Counsel for his defence.

[ARTICLE VII.]

In suits at common law, where the value in controversy shall exceed twenty dollars, the right of trial by jury shall be preserved, and no fact tried by a jury, shall be otherwise re-examined in any Court of the United States, than according to the rules of the common law.

[ARTICLE VIII.]

Excessive bail shall not be required, nor excessive fines imposed, nor cruel and unusual punishments inflicted.

[ARTICLE IX.]

The enumeration in the Constitution, of certain rights, shall not be construed to deny or disparage others retained by the people.

[ARTICLE X.]

The powers not delegated to the United States by the Constitution, nor prohibited by it to the States, are reserved to the States respectively, or to the people.

ARTICLE XI.*

The Judicial power of the United States shall not be construed to extend to any suit in law or equity, com-

* The eleventh amendment to the Constitution of the United States was proposed to the legislatures of the several States by the Third Congress on the 5th of March, 1794; and was declared in a message from the President to Congress, dated the 8th of January, 1798, to have been ratified by the legislatures of three-fourths of the States.

menced or prosecuted against one of the United States
by Citizens of another State, or by Citizens or Subjects of any Foreign State.

ARTICLE XII.*

The electors shall meet in their respective states and
vote by ballot for President and Vice-President, one of
whom, at least, shall not be an inhabitant of the same
state with themselves; they shall name in their ballots
the person voted for as President, and in distinct ballots
the person voted for as Vice-President, and they shall
make distinct lists of all persons voted for as President, and of all persons voted for as Vice-President,
and of the number of votes for each, which lists they
shall sign and certify, and transmit sealed to the seat
of the government of the United States, directed to the
President of the Senate;—The President of the Senate
shall, in presence of the Senate and House of Representatives, open all the certificates and the votes shall
then be counted;—The person having the greatest
number of votes for President, shall be the President,
if such number be a majority of the whole number of
Electors appointed; and if no person have such majority, then from the persons having the highest numbers
not exceeding three on the list of those voted for as
President, the House of Representatives shall choose
immediately, by ballot, the President. But in choosing
the President, the votes shall be taken by states, the
representation from each state having one vote; a

* The twelfth amendment to the Constitution of the United States
was proposed to the legislatures of the several States by the Eighth
Congress, on the 12th of December, 1803, in lieu of the original third
paragraph of the first section of the second article; and was declared
in a proclamation of the Secretary of State, dated the 25th of September, 1804, to have been ratified by the legislatures of three-fourths of
the States.

quorum for this purpose shall consist of a member or members from two-thirds of the states, and a majority of all the states shall be necessary to a choice. And if the House of Representatives shall not choose a President whenever the right of choice shall devolve upon them, before the fourth day of March next following, then the Vice-President shall act as President, as in the case of the death or other constitutional disability of the President.—The person having the greatest number of votes as Vice-President, shall be the Vice-President, if such number be a majority of the whole number of Electors appointed, and if no person have a majority, then from the two highest numbers on the list, the Senate shall choose the Vice-President; a quorum for the purpose shall consist of two-thirds of the whole number of Senators, and a majority of the whole number shall be necessary to a choice. But no person constitutionally ineligible to the office of President shall be eligible to that of Vice-President of the United States.

ARTICLE XIII.*

SECTION 1. Neither slavery nor involuntary servitude, except as a punishment for crime whereof the party shall have been duly convicted, shall exist within the United States, or any place subject to their jurisdiction.

SECTION 2. Congress shall have power to enforce this article by appropriate legislation.

* The thirteenth amendment to the Constitution of the United States was proposed to the legislatures of the several States by the Thirty-eighth Congress, on the 1st of February, 1865, and was declared, in a proclamation of the Secretary of State, dated the 18th of December, 1865, to have been ratified by the legislatures of twenty-seven of the thirty-six States.

ARTICLE XIV.*

SECTION 1. All persons born or naturalized in the United States, and subject to the jurisdiction thereof, are citizens of the United States and of the State wherein they reside. No State shall make or enforce any law which shall abridge the privileges or immunities of citizens of the United States; nor shall any State deprive any person of life, liberty, or property, without due process of law; nor deny to any person within its jurisdiction the equal protection of the laws.

SECTION 2. Representatives shall be apportioned among the several States according to their respective numbers, counting the whole number of persons in each State, excluding Indians not taxed. But when the right to vote at any election for the choice of electors for President and Vice-President of the United States, Representatives in Congress, the Executive and Judicial officers of a State, or the members of the Legislature thereof, is denied to any of the male inhabitants of such State, being twenty-one years of age, and citizens of the United States, or in any way abridged, except for participation in rebellion, or other crime, the basis of representation therein shall be reduced in the proportion which the number of such male citizens shall bear to the whole number of male citizens twenty-one years of age in such State.

SECTION 3. No person shall be a Senator or Representative in Congress, or elector of President and Vice-President, or hold any office, civil or military, under

---

* The fourteenth amendment to the Constitution of the United States was proposed to the legislatures of the several States by the Thirty-ninth Congress, on the 16th of June, 1866, and was declared, in a proclamation of the Secretary of State, dated the 28th of July, 1868, to have been ratified by the legislatures of thirty of the thirty-six States.

the United States, or under any State, who, having previously taken an oath, as a member of Congress, or as an officer of the United States, or as a member of any State legislature, or as an executive or judicial officer of any State, to support the. Constitution of the United States, shall have engaged in insurrection or rebellion against the same, or given aid or comfort to the enemies thereof. But Congress may by a vote of two-thirds of each House, remove such disability.

SECTION 4. The validity of the public debt of the United States authorized by law, including debts incurred for payment of pensions and bounties for services in suppressing insurrection or rebellion, shall not be questioned. But neither the United States nor any State shall assume or pay any debt or obligation incurred in aid of insurrection or rebellion against the United States, or any claim for the loss or emancipation of any slave; but all such debts, obligations and claims shall be held illegal and void.

SECTION 5. The Congress shall have power to enforce, by appropriate legislation, the provisions of this article.

ARTICLE XV.*

SECTION 1. The right of citizens of the United States to vote shall not be denied or abridged by the United States or by any State on account of race, color, or previous conditions of servitude—

SECTION 2. The Congress shall have power to enforce this article by appropriate legislation.

* The fifteenth amendment to the Constitution of the United States was proposed to the legislatures of the several States by the Fortieth Congress on the 27th of February, 1869, and was declared, in a proclamation of the Secretary of State, dated March 30, 1870, to have been ratified by the legislatures of twenty-nine of the thirty-seven States.

And a More Perfect Society of Nations 149

ARTICLE XVI.*

The Congress shall have power to lay and collect taxes on incomes, from whatever source derived, without apportionment among the several States, and without regard to any census or enumeration.

ARTICLE XVII.†

(1) The Senate of the United States shall be composed of two Senators from each State, elected by the people thereof, for six years; and each Senator shall have one vote. The electors in each State shall have the qualifications requisite for electors of the most numerous branch of the State Legislatures.

(2) When vacancies happen in the representation of any State in the Senate, the executive authority of such State shall issue writs of election to fill such vacancies: *Provided,* That the legislature of any State may empower the executive thereof to make temporary appointment until the people fill the vacancies by election as the legislature may direct.

(3) This amendment shall not be so construed as to affect the election or term of any Senator chosen before it becomes valid as part of the Constitution.

* The sixteenth amendment to the Constitution of the United States was proposed to the legislatures of the several States by the Sixty-first Congress on the 12th of July, 1909, and was declared, in an announcement by the Secretary of State, dated February 25, 1913, to have been ratified by the legislatures of thirty-eight of the forty-eight States.

† The seventeenth amendment to the Constitution of the United States was proposed to the legislatures of the several States by the Sixty-second Congress on the 16th day of May, 1912, and was declared, in an announcement by the Secretary of State, dated May 31, 1913, to have been ratified by the legislatures of thirty-six of the forty-eight States.